From Go to Whoa

Training your own horse!

From Go to Whoa

Copyright © 2019 by Pam Neal

ISBN: 9780648542605

First Printing, 2019

Photo credits:

ACE Photography, Nicole Wilson. Ev Lagoon Photography.

DISCLAIMER

Please note that Pam Neal will not accept any responsibility whatsoever for any loss, damage, injury, etc. caused for whatever reason, in any location connected with the book, "From Go to Whoa – Training your own horse" in any way.

Please note that:

Working with horses is an inherently dangerous practice and horses are incredibly unpredictable animals. Persons attempting to follow any suggestion from Pam Neal or any of her associates, **in hand or ridden,** will do so at their own risk and assume full responsibility for themselves, their horses, and any others in the vicinity. In utilizing any of the methods, practices, etc. for horsemanship suggested by Pam Neal or any of her associates, there is no guarantee of success or safety for human or horse.

Pam Neal assumes no responsibility for errors or omissions in the contents of this book.

In no event shall Pam Neal be liable for any special, direct, indirect, consequential, or incidental damages or any damages whatsoever, arising out of or in connection with the use of this book or the contents of this book.

From Go to Whoa
Training your own horse

This book has been written out of my love for helping riders reach their goals in training their own horses.

Over my 30 years of breeding, training and showing some fantastic horses, coaching youth, amateur, select amateur riders and the odd trainer, I came to learn along the way that there is a need for riders that live remotely and cannot get to regular lessons or clinics.

I began my web page for Remote Horse and Rider Training because I wanted to give these riders the chance to learn and know how to train their own horses. I started writing up some lessons and articles on training the western breeds horse on my webpage for riders that live remotely and the not so remote riders that wish they had a trainer available when sometimes things don't go to plan.

All riders should know that they *can* train their own horses with the right tools in their tool box, it really isn't rocket science. I decided then to put my experience of over 3 decades of training and breeding into a book that I could share with everyone that has an interest in training their own horse either out of necessity or pure passion.

Cheers,
Pam Neal.

Table of Contents

Choosing the right horse for YOU

Before you go to the great expense of buying a horse, you need to evaluate what will you be doing with that horse. Make no mistake, you need to really be honest with yourself as this is a huge commitment. Ask yourself what size and age of horse would work best for you as well.

Okay you have just fallen in love with a flashy looking equine and now what? What do you want to achieve and is THIS the horse for you? Are you going to be using the horse for western pleasure, trail, hunter under saddle, western riding, reining, western dressage, are you going to ride at all? Will you be interested in halter, lead trail and lunge-line?

You really do have to give this some thought and do some research before you put your hand in your pocket. I say this mainly for new "Western" riders' out there that are just coming into the western industry. I gather people that are already in the western industry know exactly what type of horse they are after.

What about this horse's temperament? Quiet, feisty, pushy, amenable, or grumpy? If you aren't comfortable with horses, don't get a pushy horse, as you will find it ruling you and not the other way around. If you are planning to just trail ride, don't buy an eventing horse.

If you don't have horse experience then do not buy a young horse and try to train it unless you are prepared to bring on-board a professional trainer who can help you with every stage. It is really a toxic cocktail when you pair a newbie human with a newbie equine. Wait until you have more experience or you may find yourself paying the price for your mistakes – such as injuries to you and your horse because you did not know what you were doing.

Take an experienced friend with you or pay for a professional trainer to check the horse out with you or for you. Better they help you assess the horse so you don't wind up over horsed (buying a horse that is way too much for you to handle).

Your experienced friend can also ride the horse for you to assess if it would work for you. If the current owner is riding the horse, and they insist you don't need to try the horse – run, don't walk as far away as you can, and keep looking.

Choosing a horse that is going to suit you and your budget is harder than you think.

The Western breeds industry has many new members every year that have come over from a different discipline usually from the English Riding discipline like Dressage, Adult Riders, Jumping, Pony Club. They welcome you guys with open arms, they want you to be with them for many years and be a happy camper, they don't want to see you leaving or letting your membership run out because in the end, the horse you picked was just not suited to what you brought it for.

Look for the right conformation for the job

Today's western performance horse is an exceptional athlete. Whatever your passion may be – western pleasure and all the various different classes that come along with that. Whether your passion is cowboy dressage, extreme trail, cutting or reining, team roping or steer wrestling. There's a horse out there that can do the job for you. However, it is crucial that you understand the different demands of each of these sports so that the right horse is selected for the job.

11

For example, there are significant differences in conformation and body type depending on the performance discipline. Cutting horses that are bred for agility, tend to be smaller and not as heavily muscled as the rodeo and roping horses that must add power and strength to the equation. Barrel racing horses must have speed and agility to successfully perform, while western pleasure show horses must have a less stockier body type to perform at very slow gaits that display a flat knee action and a strong, deep natural drive from behind.

Don't think you're getting a great deal because the horse you bought was dirt cheap.

Unlike shopping for shoes or some piece of clothing that you have snagged at an awesome bargain price, you can't buy horses like that – unless you want hard work, tears and worse still be badly injured. Do you know, there is usually a fairly good reason why that horse you think you are going to get for a bargain basement price is so cheap.

I have and still am approached by riders looking for a new horse, when asked how much they are willing to spend 80% of them tell me they don't want to go over $5,000.00.

A good quality horse in mind, body and spirit for that price is a hen with teeth! (*as rare as*).

When looking for a new prospect take someone that knows you and knows what they are looking at in a horse.

Try to take someone you know and trust that has experience and a good eye for a type of horse. Even if you have to pay for a set of professional eyes, take them with you, if they happen to comment that the horse is not suitable for you or whatever your discipline is, listen to their professional advice, they have been around the block a few times and their radar for shonky deals will be primed up.

Take your time, Rome wasn't built in a day.

It's like anything in life really – don't buy the first horse you see. Shop around, ask trainers and breeders if they know of anything about that would suit your needs. If they don't, let them know that you are interested and if they could keep you in mind.

Don't judge a book by its cover!

Don't buy a horse because you love its colour.

Just because you love the colour doesn't mean this particular horse is the one for you. Too many people buy horses because of colour, coat pattern such as paints and appaloosas. Horse's do not go well because they have a beautiful coat pattern or they are your favourite colour.

I nearly made this mistake myself once…

– don't buy a horse just on the fact that it is a brother or sister to the one you may have lost due to death from illness, injury or any other misfortune. Horse's, just like humans, they are individuals and it's not always going to work out that the brother or sister is going to be just as good dependant on the lineage.

13

Do your research on the lineage, not forgetting the mare's lineage when researching, it seems that the dam's heritability has a very specific meaning in genetics. There has been some research done by a team in China and Australia titled "Potential role of maternal lineage in the thoroughbred breeding strategy" which you can read more about on PubMed. It examined the relative genetic influence of the sire and dam in racing performance as documented in terms of lifetime earnings. The researcher's finding was that "elite" (top-winning) sires bred to elite dams were more likely to produce elite offspring, and likewise poor sires bred to poor dams produced poor offspring. But the kicker was that poor dams bred to elite sires tended to produce poor offspring. So, a great sire can't compensate for a poor dam, but a great dam can produce a great performer with a poor-quality sire.

These researchers found that 14% of the variation in performance among horses could be attributed to the genetic influence of the dam, but only 3.5% to the sire. To me, that's a good enough reason to check out the dam and not just the sire when looking for your perfect, four-legged partner. I believe a larger percentage of people put more research into which sire they would like their horse to be by, not giving much thought to the dam.

Keeping your horse in tip-top Health

If you own a horse, you are probably aware of the time and money needed to properly care for it.

Feeding

I personally like feeding horses the "Oldtimers" way. Especially if you can source organic grains – no pesticides or herbicides included.

You can choose to use oats or barley. If you are feeding Oats make sure you are getting them crimped or crushed *just* before feeding up. Or if you prefer to feed out Barley, soak it overnight and then drain the juice through a sieve right before feeding up. Buying any grain that is crimped or crushed when purchased will have virtually zero nutritious value, who knows how long ago it was crimped or crushed leaching out all of the important nutrition. To get the most possible nutrition you can from these grains, crush or crimp just before feeding.

I like to mix the oats or, if using barley in with oaten chaff.

Multi-Vitamins & Essential Supplements

Using a good quality multi vitamin/mineral in their daily feed will help make this mixture a complete nutrient dense feed especially if you incorporate a small square of Lucerne hay and some good quality pasture hay.

I personally can't go past HI Form Australia for good quality, human grade, organic products. The main thing here is making sure your horse is getting the vitamins and minerals it needs.

Using a good quality pasture hay is great. I like to wait for an hour after they have finished their hard feed before I feed out their hay. This gets them a little bit further into the night, keeping their digestive tract working for as long as possible. It is not good for horses to go for hours without any food going through their system. Studies have shown that this is a major cause of stomach and intestinal ulcers.

Tip: Purchase a hay bag that has the smaller diamond or square webbing in the front section of the canvas bag for these two reasons:

1. Hay bags are safer than straight out large open diamond webbing hay nets. I have seen a horse or two pawing at the nets looking to get more hay out of them when they are left hanging in the stables empty, getting a hoof caught in the net. It is not a pretty sight and is dangerous.

2. A hay bag with a square mesh front slowing the horse's eating habits down, making the hay last longer, that is hugely beneficial to the stabled horse.

Providing your horse, a well-balanced diet is one of the most important aspects of good equine health.

The age and workload of your horse will also depend on how much you feed out. For example, a young horse needs extra supplements included in his diet to help protect his joints and growth plates at a crucial growth time.

• Hi Form BreedPlus formula has been specifically designed for breeding stock. Broodmares, breeding stallions, foals and yearlings. This formula is designed to support the growth and development of the foetus and young horse, the mare through her pregnancy and lactation stages as well as the servicing stallion. Research has shown the developmental orthopaedic diseases such as OCD, cervical vertebra, malformations, angular deformities, contracted tendons and

16

physitis can be caused by many factors such as genetic predisposition, management practices, diseases and dietary influences. (Foster n.d.)

An older horse, a ridden horse on the other hand will require different supplements, however, they may also need extra supplements for maintenance of bone and joints.

It's also worth knowing what types of supplements I use and recommend for rehabilitation of your horse coming back from an injury or illness.

Ideal for show horses.

- **Hi Form CompletaVite** is the perfect daily supplement for horses in light work, retired horses or those having a spell. CompletaVite will provide a lovely, healthy, shiny coat and condition, ideal for the show horse.
- This formula is very economical and ideal for those competing irregularly or starting a younger horse in training. CompletaVite can also assist in horses being spelled over winter, with extra Vitamin C and added herbs.
- Superior skin health and coat shine Formulated to suit show horses, horses in light work, retired or spelling horses. Economical and designed to improve utilisation of dietary nutrients and assist overall health and condition. (Foster n.d.)
- **Hi Form TopLine** Increase muscle tone and top line. A natural way to achieve top line in just six weeks, gaining that performance advantage you need to win.
- Contains amino acids including L-Arginine. Excellent for horses with a poor appetite or in a run-down condition. TopLine DOES NOT contain whey powder, which is used in almost all muscle building products for humans and horses. Whey protein is the protein that is derived from whey, which is a by-product of the cheese made from cow's milk! Horses are herbivores, whey may be acceptable for humans, but I do

not feel comfortable feeding it to horses. Human studies published in Nov 2011 stated 'whey protein may affect glucose metabolism and muscle protein synthesis. However, the evidence for a clinical efficacy is not strong enough to make final recommendations with respect to a specific dose and the duration of supplementation'. Other supporting amino acids, herbs, specific B-Group vitamins and trace elements work extremely powerfully in a synergistic way,TopLine does NOT contain FISH products or other by-products which are totally unsuitable for herbivores! (Foster n.d.)

Aches and Pains – Injuries

- **Hi Form ProflamAid Plus** contains vitamins and minerals that have a role in wound healing and the maintenance of normal healthy joints. The nutrients contained in these formulas have a role in general metabolism and red blood cell formation, act as an anti-oxidant and assist in maintaining normal nitrogen balance in tissues.

- **Hi Form EquiGesic Plus** in a league of its own! EquiGesic Plus has the most amazing pain relief properties allowing osteoarthritic cases to remain in work, Osteoarthritis is a very common condition and if managed the life of the performance horse or happy hacker can be extended. Activity is the number 1 key to managing this condition, so it makes absolute sense to use a safe well researched formula. The EquiGesic Plus also has many other amazing attributes such as it's very strong antioxidant effect and exceptionally high absorption and utilisation rate, making this not only highly effective but also fast acting. The EquiGesic Plus contains the following ingredients: Curcumin C3 Complex patented extract exclusive to Hi Form Australia Pty Ltd BioPerine Patented extract (piper nigrum) exclusive to Hi Form Australia Pty Ltd Boswellia Serrata extract, Palatinose plus Essential Fatty acids

Rehabilitation

BIOEQUUS ™ By Hi Form Australia
- Supporting the Gut Microbiome
- Contains two Glycoproteins – GlycomaxTM
- Lactoferrin & Glycomax TM Immunoglobulins
- For symptomatic relief of Ulcers

- For the removal of Mycotoxins
- Lactobacillus plantarum may help to relieve intestinal inflammation
- Assists in the management and relief from symptoms of allergies
- Assists in the management of Candida infections. For the treatment and symptomatic relief of pain and discomfort from gastritis
- Helps to reduce the side effects of antibiotic use, and in the occurrence of diarrhoea during and after antibiotic administration
- Helps to restore and maintain health in the digestive system, the bacterial flora and the mucosal function

The synergy between prebiotics and probiotics supported by the gut soothing certified organic herb extracts, helps to restore a healthy balance and benefits metabolism in the digestive system. Horses love this formula and the BioEquus helps to maintain a healthy bacterial flora and has a beneficial impact on metabolic processes. BioEquus will assist in maintaining a healthy gut microbiome.

Feeding a high roughage diet is essential for a healthy digestive system and gut microbiome.

ProflamAid Plus is also an ideal supplement for rehabilitation. Terrific for wound healing, colic, navicular, absolutely everything!

The next supplement I will add on to the rehab list would be TopLine it will help increase a sick horse's appetite and help in re-building muscle.

Vaccination

Vaccines have an important role in preventing diseases. They also have had an important role on eradicating disease. If you think back to the Equine Influenza outbreak in 2007 in Australia, vaccination had an important role in preventing spread of disease and eradicating the disease from Australia. Put your horse on a regular schedule for their vaccinations such as

- Equivac 2in1 (Tetanus and Strangles). **Tetanus** is caused by the production of toxins from a soil borne bacterium that can contaminate any wound. There is definitely a high fatality risk of tetanus, it is therefore important that your horse is up to date with this vaccination. DON'T wait for a wound to occur until you vaccinate! **Strangles** is caused by infection with a bacteria *Streptococcus equip Subspecies equi.* Highly contagious, spreads with *(in contact)* with other horses that have the virus.

- **Hendra Virus.** The virus has bats as its natural reservoir. The virus can be spread to horses. Dogs, ferrets and cats are also known to be affected but, in these species, it may not cause symptoms.

- **Equine Herpes Virus (EHV).** Most commonly associated with upper respiratory tract infections (colds), however, they are on occasion associated with abortion in broodmares and paralysis in horses.

Other viruses that are found in the United States and other parts of the world are:

- West Nile Virus
- Rabies
- 2-Way or 3-Way Sleeping Sickness
- Potomac Horse Fever

For further information on these you can source more information from www.valleyvet.com.

Keep a log of all of your vaccinations so that you will know when the various vaccinations are due. This can also help if there is ever a situation where the vet needs to know of previous vaccinations.

While your vet probably keeps records of this, it is a good idea for you to have them as well.

Farrier

Keep an eye on your horses' feet, especially when you are turning them out for the winter. Whether you're into barefoot trimming or shoeing, they need their feet seen to.

1. Take their shoes off before turning out. (Some may need to stay shod depending on the condition of their feet).
2. Keep getting the farrier out every 6 or 8 weeks for trimming. Poorly kept feet can lead to a variety of lameness problems, and can be very painful for your horse.

Dentist

I can't stress this enough – find a really good equine dentist. I was blessed to find and hang on to what I claim was the best dentist in Australia! I can't tell you how many horses came to me with really, *really* bad mouths. It's no wonder some were cantankerous until they had the correct work done in their mouths. It's not enough to just have a rasp run over the teeth, sure, it helps take the sharpness off but does nothing much else.

Worming

Keep your horse's digestive tract healthy by de-worming on a regular basis. Failure to do this can result in your horse having an infestation of worms that can result in significant harm.

There are quite a lot of tell-tale signs that your horse may have worms, and without going into all of the different species of worms, where they live in your horse and the extent of damage they can do, you can usually tell.

- If one is dull and bleached in the coat
- tucked up in the flank
- potbellied
- lethargic
- pale in the gums and under lids of eyes
- won't put on weight no matter how much feed you put into them
- continually scratching their butt at every possible opportunity, they get.

I once had a horse arrive that was definitely not a pin-up for the healthiest looking horse. She was "spindly", tucked up even after two weeks of the delivery date. I always insisted that the owners wormed their horses at least two weeks before arrival, I would worm them again two weeks after arrival, which I did for this mare. She had a couple of little red worms in the dung so I re-wormed a week later – same thing, a few reddies. I had my vet do a dung test which came back positive to infestation of worms. The vet had to come back and the mare had to be stomach tubed, she had a close shave with nearly having to have a blood transfusion. I couldn't see the poop for all of the worms a day or two after the drenching!

This was a costly exercise, 100% more for the owner than a simple worming routine.

Weanling handling

It takes a long time from inception to conception. Nearly 12 months once the mare is bred.

From foaling day until the day you can ride your pride and joy can be anything from two to four years depending on the circumstances – whether your horse will be in training with a professional as a two and three-year-old or maybe you just don't want to ride him until he is nearing his four year old year. This adds up to five years of waiting.

It's nice to have the babies at least learning the ropes with ground work if not getting out to the shows. It does wonders for their temperament if it is approached the right way.

Start Simply

Whether you have bought yourself a young weanling or have bred one on the farm, it's going to go a long way if you start slowly and simply with them when you do bring them in from the paddock.

You may not be interested in showing your baby however, the importance of bringing them in, introducing them to a stable, if not already – introduce hard feeding, visits with the farrier and as long yearlings the dentist goes a long way to getting them to the breaking in stage.

Make all of these things and more – routine.

Mistakes are often made in the first training sessions. This happens because foals and weanlings are small and it is easy for people to handle them incorrectly.

The too much loving and buckets of treats, where the little cutie turns into a very difficult, disrespectful horse who assumes position as the "Alpha" in the relationship. Then you have the "Before this fella gets too big, I'll show him who is boss". This can often lead to the horse becoming distrustful of humans and flighty. The handler never gives it a thought that the problem was man-made, the horse gets blamed. "This horse is crazy, and can't be trained!".

Using the mare to help out

Provided you have bred your own mare and have her available to use, it's a great idea to use her to your advantage when working with her young foal. If you have bought the foal from outside of your property already weaned, hopefully, it should know how to lead and be loaded on a float.

Here is what I do when I bring my foals up with their mothers:

A week or two before I send the mare back to the paddock without the bub, I begin teaching the foal to lead along with its mother, it makes it a bit easier on both foal and handler if you start this while mum is still in the picture. While the mare is still helping out with ensuring the foal is relaxed because mum's there so all is well in the world.

I hook on the lead rope and use what I call a "bum rope". Stand slightly off to the side of the foal and put light pressure on the lead rein and hold. This will usually put the foal off balance a bit because I am pulling to the one side. As soon as the foal takes a step to get his balance back again I release my hold on the lead.

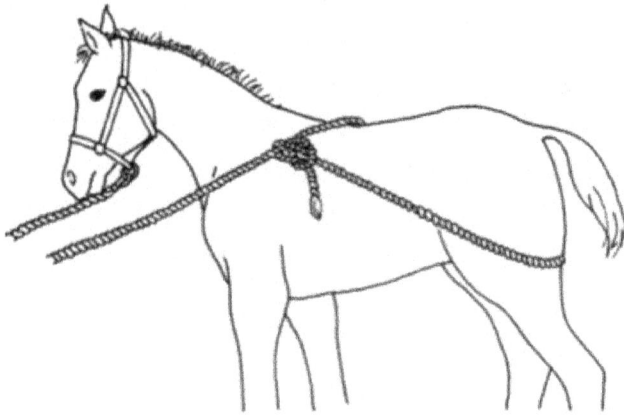

I reward with a little rub on the neck, but I don't go overboard, just enough to instil confidence and let him know that I'm not out to eat him.

I repeat this action over and over again until he learns the art of moving toward light pressure. My release of the lead when he moves toward me is his reward.

Once I have the foal responding to me by walking toward me with light pressure, it's time for the mare to leave. Once the mare is out of the picture and the weanling has settled in a bit, I begin to teach them various things that all weanlings need to know.

- how to tie up
- sacking out
- have their feet picked up
- back-up
- introduce a rug
- lead beside you at a walk and jog
- stand quietly
- introduce them to the float

The more you work on these repetitively at a young age, the better they will be when it's time to think about being broken in.

Tying Up

The first three to four weeks I don't exactly tie the weaners up, I put the lead through a ring on the front of the stable door in the breezeway and I will hold it while I brush them, rub them down, pick their feet up etc. When they move back, forth, side-ways whatever, I will go with them and let the lead run through the ring.

When it is time to actually tie them up, they seem to handle it really naturally. If, however, they don't, you can use a piece of old inner tubing from a bicycle tyre to tie them up to. The inner tubing will absorb the shock of a sudden jerk. I have even used a "body rope" around the heart girth, run through between the legs and through the ring on the halter, then I will tie them to the inner tubing that is fastened to the ring on the door.

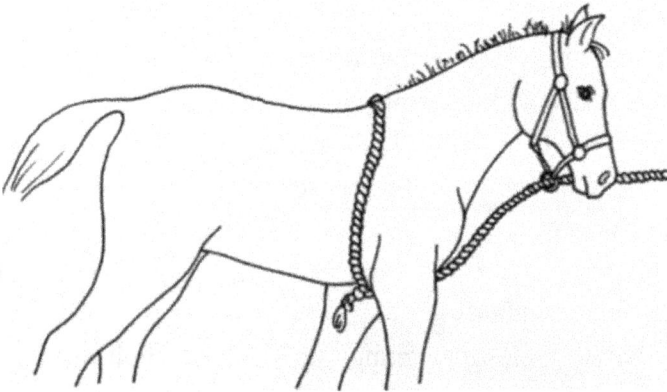

Sacking Out

Sacking out is a method used to desensitize a horse to potentially frightening situations or objects.

It is a process that, done properly, teaches a horse to not fear certain objects or situations, and, over time can be used to teach a horse to stop and listen to its handler in any potentially frightening situation, thus, in effect, to assess the situation instead of immediately acting upon its fight or flight instinct. This is a method used to get a horse used to a frightening stimulus while he remains in a relaxed state. It is commonly done with things that will be touching the horse, such as saddle pads, towels or stable blankets. Even using your hands running over a foal or unhandled horse is the beginnings of "sacking out".

You can sack any horse out at any age and at any point in the horse's training.

I will start sacking horses out from their weanling year. Naturally it won't be the same as if I was sacking out a yearling or older horse but none-the-less, I start them young.

I don't like to use anything noisy or crackly to start with, I use a bit of cloth or an old towel. I hold the towel at one end and rub the foal with it. Eventually, I turn that rub into a rhythmic, patting motion all over the foal's body.

You might like to be in the stable when you begin sacking out, some of them do run around quite a bit when you start waving the towel around but don't stop the rhythm you have, even if you are nowhere near your foal's body parts, keep sacking out and follow them slowly around until they settle and you can re-connect.

Eventually, you should be able to tap the towel all the way down the legs, under the belly, between the front and back legs and over the neck and body.

When it comes to sacking out the face, I will rub them with the towel ensuring that there is a fair bit hanging down, this gets a response from the foal at first, then they settle down once they realise it's not going to hurt them. You can't fix what isn't broke so having the towel flapping a little and getting that response will help you desensitise their reaction, just be a lot quieter and a tad gentler on the foals.

Later, when they are able to handle the towel, I tie some thick tape around a heavy paper feed bag to make a handle, the other end is fanned out, I sack them out with that but not until they are well and truly over the hype of having a scary towel flapped all over them.

Remember count a rhythm and continue that rhythm even if you are not touching the foal's body, this will help them realise you're not going to hurt them. Don't come in with any sneaky one's between a long break. You might think to stop swinging the towel if the foal wants to tear off on you – you have lost the rhythm, when you start up again it can startle them, they may have thought it was all over but then you come back in with the towel.

Picking up the feet

Now that they are well versed with the towel flapping around all over their body you can start rubbing them down with your bare hand. Moving down toward the feet. Rub your hands all over them starting on the neck and body at first, keep rubbing them so that they know you are there. It's never a good idea to go straight to a horse's back leg to pick it up. Always run your hand down his body, including his hip and continue down his leg that you will be picking up. Stand in close to them as well, if they do happen to want to kick out at you it is better that they can only bump you away rather than give you a good kick with the extension of their leg. Don't rush into rubbing their ears and face, leave this area to last when they have had a chance to settle into you handling them.

Start by gently but firmly holding your hand around their cannon bone then wait and see what sort of response you get from that, if there is no bad response, run your hand down to the fetlock, go ahead and pick up the leg and just rub the sole of the hoof. Moving on, you can then tap the sole of the hoof. Place the leg back down and give your bub a pat to solidify that nothing is wrong.

Repeat this on the off-side front leg, remember, horses are one sided so you may have to go back to square one for a bit until the information hits home.

You can stick with the front legs for a few days if you don't think that they are ready for the back legs before you go there. If they are pretty laid back, go on back rubbing their hips, down their legs and repeat the process.

If, by chance, you have a timid one that is a bit frightened of what you are doing back there you could use a soft rope as an extension of your hand, put it around the bottom of the back leg, gathering up both ends of the rope put some pressure on it so that the foals leg comes forward and off the ground.

If this is the case with your foal, that they are a bit frightened, go slow, take your time at this until your foal accepts it.

Be prepared for some short, sharp, jabs as he tries to free his leg from the rope.

Backing

I give a voice command "back" to the foal and as I do, I apply pressure on the noseband of the halter. Bump rhythmically on the lead with short jerks. I don't try and hold a solid pulling on the lead, this tends to panic them, you always have to give them an "out", if they feel there is no give they can panic.

Push the weaner on the shoulder, I use the flat of my hand first (always start with the lesser amount of pressure), if they don't respond, I make a fist, bend my index finger and poke them in the shoulder until they move back. All I ask is one step for now, I don't push the envelope at all when I am teaching babies.

Introduce the rug

Because I have been sacking out on a daily basis with the towel, rubbing my hands all over his body and down his legs, lifting his feet and patting him down a bit, he shouldn't be too perturbed about the rug being introduced.

I grab a light sheet, roll it up, place it on their wither and play around with it there for a bit. I will bring the rug down toward their hips and rump then bring it back up again placing it purposefully on their wither with a drop of about 6 inches so they know I'm doing something back here.

It doesn't take long and I'm able to unravel the rug (make sure your leg straps are secured to the rug, don't have them criss-crossed just before you go to drop them down beside the foal's legs). I will rub the rug around a little bit to see if I get a response from the foal. By now they should be pretty good to handle around their legs so unclip the back-leg strap, feed it between the back legs and do it up (for now don't cross the straps over). Go around and do the same on the off side.

Lesson in leading at the walk and trot

The Walk

I usually start this lesson in a smaller area like the round yard, I use the rubber rail to hold them in place, right beside me so they can't run off in the opposite direction. After a few successful attempts I put them alongside a sturdy closed in wall in the arena.

Starting at a walk, I will position myself at their shoulder, I work on keeping the foal walking with me. Every so often cueing him to whoa with voice and body language. I will tilt back slightly in my torso as I say whoa, this is a visual cue to help them. I stay with the walk until I have him walking and stopping in both directions.

If I have problems with him not wanting to walk beside me, I rub the end of the lunge whip on their hip, if that doesn't do the trick in getting him in alongside me, I tap the end of the lunge whip and cluck.

Note: So, I haven't got a little fire cracker on the end of the lead shank when starting this lesson, I take them into the round yard and set them free, just let them play for a bit and investigate the area. I let them settle down so that they can concentrate more on the lesson. If the foal is stabled full-time while in the process of learning various things, it gives them some freedom time.

The Jog or Trot

When you are ready to work on them jogging beside you, if you tilt slightly forward and cluck, this is the cue to jog on, it probably won't happen off the bat but that is the cue I use regardless.

Once again holding the lunge whip in the hand furthest away from them, give them the jog cue and start rubbing the end of the whip on their hip, if they don't trot off tap them on the hip with the end of the whip.

One of two things usually happen here:

1. They get a fright and run flat out past you
2. They baulk and won't come forward at all

Be patient with them, take a breath and start over, as soon as they take a respectable trot off for you, that's enough, that's all you can ask for. They usually come back the next day having slept on it, all they want to do is trot...funny buggers.

Stand quietly

I don't worry at all where they plant their feet as long as they whoa and as long as it's for at least 10 to 15 seconds. I usually work on the stand quietly lesson on the way back to the stable. As I am walking back with them, I'll ask them to whoa and stand quietly for 10 seconds (this doesn't mean allowing them to graze on your arm or chew on the lead). Then I will cue them to walk on.

If you tried for a longer stand time in the beginning you are probably going to get frustrated with them pretty quick. Remember they are babies and don't have a very long concentration span or learning span. If you get a few goodies out of lots of baddies, that's not a problem, don't make an issue out of it.

Teach the halter pose

Once your baby is standing quietly for those few seconds on his way back to the stable, you can start adding to it and including a bit of finesse to him standing up.

Start teaching him to stand and pose for the halter class. You can start doing this by using the correct pressure on the halter. To move the hind feet, pull down slightly, pull down and slightly toward you to move the offside rear forward, if you want to move it back it's down and toward your horse. I like to use the word "set" just before I apply the pressure.

Moving the front feet, lift the horses head slightly and toward you, this will encourage them to bring the off front forward. Move their head up and away from you to put it back.

Initially, at home I will point my toe as like a plan B. I don't like to touch their feet with my toe but sometimes it is necessary until they get the picture. Try to avoid it but if you need to for a back-up then point your toe as you use the other cues. Eventually, you can stop pointing the toe but I like to know that it's a "thing" just in case nothing else is working. Don't touch them in the class though, that's a no, no.

Introduction of the float

There's no time like the present! Don't think you have to wait until they are older, now is the time and it's a great time at that.

I bring a double float over by the stables and leave it there for a week or two beside the foal's day yard.

While it's sitting there, about the 4th day in, I will bring another horse over and load it right beside the foal's day yard so he can see what's going on and to get him used to the clang, bang noise. This way they get used to it being there, by the time you're ready for float training they won't be jumping out of their skin when it suddenly appears out of nowhere.

I like to have some feed just inside the loading ramp, I will stand the foal at the loading ramp, let them chill out there for a little bit, if they get bored and try to walk away I bring them back around in a circle, grab hold of the bucket of feed (pick something they love eating at this lesson), I will be a little way up the loading ramp with the bucket, I won't stretch my arm out to them unless I need their attention to be brought back to the bucket. Usually, the bucket gets the better of them and they stretch out to reach the goodies.

You may get a step out of them at this stage as they are stretching out, if you do, awesome but if not that's fine. If they *do* take that one step let them eat out of the bucket – the whole lot at this stage. That there to me is enough for the lesson. Watch tomorrow how much better they are at going up for that food!

I don't like to push them with this, I find the noise of them coming up the ramp can send them straight back and they get frightened by it so you don't want to take it any further than that one step on the first day.

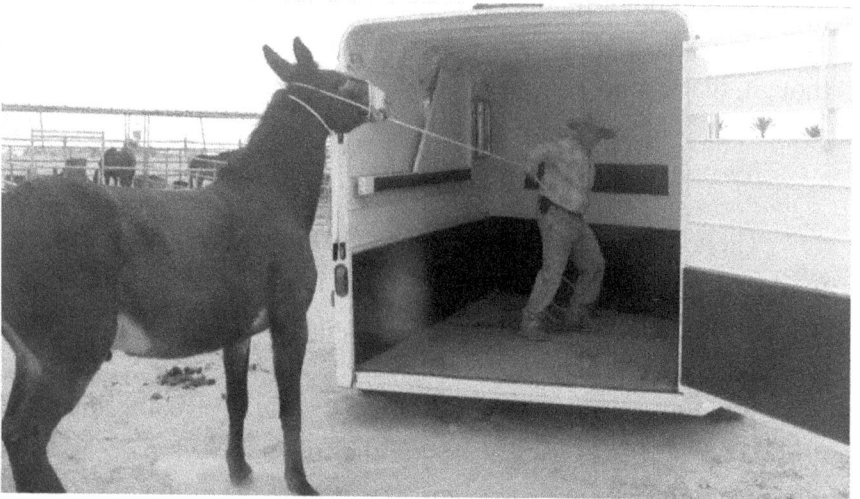

He-aw, he-aw, he-always does this to me!

I think he will be there for a while

If you have the opportunity, tie a friendly buddy up on the left side of the float. I hear you say, "why the left side of the float"? Come the day when your bub is ready to go show and he is going to be on his own it just takes a little bit of worrying out of the picture, just in-case they happen to not want to walk up a strange side.

Your single travelling horse should ALWAYS travel on the driver's side in a float.
Why:
1. Less potholes (as a rule)
2. Less friction on their legs and bodies, in case you happen to get off into the side.

The driver's side makes for a smoother ride.

Once you have got them right up into the float don't try and tie them up, just stand there with them, if there is any food left in the bucket let them stand there and finish it off.

If you can, back them off the float and end it there for the day.

I would recommend keeping this routine up daily.

You can see that you have plenty of work to do while you wait for bub to grow up.

Prepping to Show your weanling

It used to be that looking good and squaring up well were enough to be competitive in the show pen. These days, you really have to work hard to be competitive. Our weanlings and yearlings are improving out of site as far as type goes. Used to be, years ago you could easily place your ridden bred horse in a halter class without a problem of maybe winning or placing really well. Today, it's a whole new story.

Not only do you really need to do your homework on 'type', conformation etc but you need to expose a youngster to the sights and sounds he'll encounter in the show ring. Unless you do so, all of your hard work at home practicing squaring your horse up all the necessary elbow grease and shank time can go to waste, as your weanling is suddenly thrown in the deep end of stimuli around him and suddenly switches you off.

The judge won't have a chance to evaluate that dancing, prancing, stressed out bundle of nerves. You'll have wasted not only an entry fee, but also time and energy. And, you'll have made your weanling's show debut a negative experience rather than a positive one.

So, to give it your best shot at a winner here are a few things you can do to get into the line-up: -

Here comes the judge.

- Get your weanling used to standing squared up around a couple of friends that you can use as judges. Have them wear a cowboy hat, hold clipboards filled with paper. Making sure they flip the pages around in front on your weanling. Have them approach you, circle around you, practice showing your weaners teeth. Many competitors overlook this simple strategy, only to discover on show day that their weanlings don't take kindly to approaching judges, the sight and noise of shuffling papers have been known to spook even the mellowest of weanlings. Practice walking to the judge and jogging away.

Practice with other horses.

- Practice leading and lining up with other horses, get your friends if you can to bring their horses or better still, if they also have a weanling to practice with. Set up mock classes at home, get some friends and their horses to line up with you.

It pays to be observant

- While you are in the warm up pen at a show observe the other weanlings that will be in your class and pick your lead-in position whenever possible. Look at all the other weanlings and pick yourself a couple of quiet-looking weanlings. If you see one acting pretty frisky, steer clear of that one if at all possible. It can be like the Domino effect if one weanling goes off, they will all tend to go off.

I personally prefer to be the first one in…first impressions and all, plus you want to be out of the crowd as much as possible in-case one does decide to start the Domino effect.

Don't leave dressing up to the last minute

One thing I would stress you definitely do before heading off to a show is to be sure to band your weanling's mane and apply face make-up before you head out for that first show. Do lots of handling of your baby's muzzle and around the ears and eyes, starting well in advance of show day.

While you are out with your weanling in the round yard or arena, take a small set of portable clippers in your pocket. Get them out and turn them on but don't try to touch them with the clippers, just let them get used to hearing them for a week or two. From that you can build on it.

Having the clippers securely in your hand begin to touch your baby with the back-side of your hand while they are running. Do this ever so gradual and build on it. If you see that your weanling is genuinely spinning out in fear stop the procedure and go back to just turning the clippers on at a distance.

Some weanlings don't mind these procedures, but others do. Find out your weanling's tolerance levels while you still have time to solve any problems. Having sacked him out in his training will go a long way for you here.

Take nothing for granted.

- Hang some flags around and work with your weanling until he ignores them. You can hang some of them up loosely so that they go in and out with the wind and flap.
- Practice leading your weanling over varying ground surfaces, up and down gutters, over wet ground, gravel etc.
- Get your horse car, truck, tractor, motor bike ready. Once he has accepted loading into the float, take him to a show somewhere, lead him around and let him see everything that goes on there.

- Outfit your weanling in his show halter when performing all training and desensitization sessions. If you were to have him practice in his everyday halter, you'd risk not only a different level of responsiveness when he's wearing his show gear at an event, but also that he'd spook from the look and feel of an unfamiliar halter.

Judging of a halter horse is an evaluation of conformation, body condition and way of going. Each of these judging criteria can be influenced by the preparation of the horse.

Preparing a halter horse for the show pen is a combination of:
- balanced nutrition,
- daily grooming,
- strict health management,
- specific exercise programs
- superior genetics.

All of these factors are combined with more hard work and attention to detail than many people care to do, but if you have a love and feel for it, it can be very rewarding and should be lots of fun.

There are pre-requisites that proper preparation can have on a halter horse. Genetics cannot be changed and will eventually sort out the "real ones" from the pretenders. All the elbow grease and attention to detail in the world will not take an inferior horse into a world champion.

Feeding your foal for Showing

Getting the weanling in show condition is probably the most difficult prep job of all. The combination of rapid skeletal growth, selecting a proper exercise regime, and managing a hair coat that seems to change daily, makes life difficult for those showing weanlings.

From a nutrition perspective, several factors must be considered in a weanling diet. First, weanlings have specific nutrient requirements that must be satisfied in order to achieve sound growth. The first six dietary factors to consider are:

1. energy,
2. protein,
3. calcium,
4. phosphorus,
5. copper and
6. zinc.

A weanling can only eat so much feed. This limited intake will ensure that a weanling diet be concentrated with the correct nutrients. If your foal were to be fed a poorly digested, high fibre diet, it would only serve only to fill him up and give him a hay belly.

The hay/pasture component of the diet should consist of high-quality hay. Coarse stems or long (mature) seed heads indicate the hay is past the optimum nutritive value for weanlings. A good Lucerne, or Lucerne/grass mix provides a palatable source of fibre for young horses.

The amount of hay/pasture provided depends on several factors including size and weight of the weanling along with desired growth rate. In general, a weanling is fed proportionally more grain and less hay as the desired growth rate is increased. A rule of thumb for hay intake is a minimum of 1 pound of good quality hay per 100 pounds of body weight.

If you read the section on Keeping Your Horse in tip-top health you would have read that I am a true believer in the "Old Timers" way of feeding a horse. I like to feed them grains like oats or barley. I mainly feed out barley because that is what is available locally from the farmer.

I like to soak them for 24 hours. Barley along with other grains contain an anti-nutrient called phytic acid which binds with certain minerals (e.g. zinc, phosphorous, calcium and iron) and prevents them from being absorbed by the body. Phytic acid is also very hard on the digestive system. Most of the phytic acid is contained in the exterior bran and germ layers of the grain. Ironically, whole grains are much higher in minerals than polished or refined grains, but we won't receive those benefits unless we neutralize the phytic acid.

Phytic acid is also an enzyme-inhibitor which keeps the grains/seeds dormant until the conditions for germination are just right. Not only does phytic acid prevent seeds from sprouting, it also helps protect them from predators by blocking digestive enzymes so that the seeds stay untouched as they pass through the digestive tract.

Soaking or sprouting grains before feeding them out will neutralize the phytic acid and release the enzyme inhibitors, thus making them much easier to digest and making the nutrients more available.

Once soaked, I let the juice run out through the sieve I mix the barley up with chaff and for the youngsters I would add a pellet as well that is suitable for foals and yearlings. I would also add a multi vitamin/mineral supplement, joint protection supplement and a required amount of one of my favourite products, made by Hi Form Australia called Top Line. An excellent product that really works on getting any horse not just the babies build, grow and shine. Hi Form Australia were a huge part in my horses being so successful in the show pen whether it be halter or ridden. They always looked gorgeous.

So, the hard feed kept basic with all the right supplements manually included into the foal's daily feeds (see above under supplements). This is a great way to go because you can add or subtract things as you monitor the condition of the horse.

Last but not least – good quality pasture/Lucerne hay. Fed in a hay bag that has a smaller nylon mesh on the front to slow down their eating. Doing this, their hay lasts well into the night helping to keep their digestive tract working optimally.

It is very important to keep an eye on your youngsters' condition. You don't want their legs blowing out due to overfeeding.

Many people are afraid to feed young horses too much protein for fear of causing bone problems. However, mild excesses in protein intake will not cause bone problems. Instead, imbalances in mineral intake or extremely rapid growth triggered by excess energy intake are likely causes of bone anomalies.

The daily feeding should be balanced with respect to calcium and phosphorus so the weanling will get the proper amount and the correct ratio (balance) of these minerals.

At a recommended grain intake of 1 pound per month of age, this would make it necessary for the feed to contain approximately 50 ppm copper and 200 ppm zinc. For weanlings receiving larger amounts of grain, the concentration of copper and zinc can be less.

The physical form of the supplement or concentrate, whether a pellet, a supplement product, is not critical as long as the product is properly balanced and the weanlings readily consume it.

Exercising the Weanling

Many people incorrectly think a halter horse need only be fat to be successful. In fact, modern halter horses must display muscle tone. Exercise is the method of choice to achieve muscle toning. Many methods of providing forced exercise are available, including hand walking, lunging, ponying, and treadmills. Ponying is becoming increasingly popular since the horses are not being asked to constantly turn as is the case with lunging.

If you can, the use of 4-wheel ATV bike is a common one used by many horse owners. Horses quickly adapt to it and look forward to their exercise.

If the duration and intensity of exercise are too great for the individual horse, injury and weight loss can occur. On the other hand, young horses confined to stalls without adequate exercise will possess less bone mass than exercised weanlings. Any exercise program should be adjusted to the conformation and body condition of the individual horses. A single exercise program will not fit every weanling.

Grooming

Grooming can be a deal breaker in the preparation process. A thorough, vigorous daily grooming should follow the exercise program.

- A small, flexible rubber curry is an essential tool to remove dead hair and stimulate skin circulation.
- Many horse owners now use special equine vacuums to thoroughly clean the horses. Horses can be vacuumed or soft brushed to remove the dirt and flake raised by currying.
- A warm bath with mild shampoo can also be used to rinse off dirt and flake. Care should be taken to rinse the weanling thoroughly to prevent skin drying and irritation that can result if shampoo is left on the skin. Scrape excess water from the horse and allow time for drying before turning the horse loose in the stall. This is also a good time to reapply tail and mane conditioner. Allow the tail to dry completely before working out any tangles or brushing. If the tail is long, a loose French braid starting at the top of the tail minimizes hair breakage but the braid needs to be loose so as not to cause breakage.
- Tail bags are another useful means of protecting valuable tail hair.
- The hooves should be kept well-trimmed or shod. On show day, a light buffing with a fine emery cloth makes the hoof surface smooth and slick. A hoof polish or light coat of hoof oil can be applied to give the hoof a shine.
- The bridle path, ears, legs and face should all be carefully clipped prior to the show.

- A highlighter around the eyes and muzzle is a nice touch on show days.
- Ears and nostrils should be wiped out with a cloth treated with a light coat conditioner.

Finally, a beautiful hair coat with a healthy shine cannot be sprayed on. It is a product of hard work, remember, the elbow grease and preparation done in the months prior to the show.

I actually have a funny story about elbow grease. I was preparing a client's young weanling, they were relatively new to the show and preparation side of things. They called in one day to visit their girl, gasping at how good she looked and asking "How did you get her so shiny"? I explained "A lot of elbow grease"! One of them replied "Oh lovely, and where do you buy that, I should get some?" I laughed for quite some time about that one.

Preparing the Yearling

Champion Filly. Owners: Richelle & Alisha Portelli Handler: Pam Neal

Yearlings are generally easier to prepare for show than are weanlings. However, many yearlings can go through awkward stages due to growth spurts. These periods of rapid growth can leave the yearling looking poorly balanced (taller in the hindquarters) and occasionally thin. Many people equate awkward yearlings with human teenagers. Just as teenagers come in different shapes and sizes, so do yearlings. Therefore, large variations in the amount of feed necessary to prepare a halter yearling are common.

As with the weanling diet, the feed concentrate should be properly balanced with calcium, phosphorus, copper and zinc. A grain intake of 2 – 4 kg (4 – 8 pounds) per yearling per day is a fairly standard grain intake, but is variable with breed and body size. Larger amounts of grain are occasionally needed for big, scopey yearlings. If elevated levels of grain seem to be necessary, you may use alternative sources of energy.

Two energy sources commonly used are fat and soluble fibre (beet pulp). Each of these energy sources provides the yearling with readily available energy to support growth. In addition, these energy sources are safer to feed than the high starch-containing cereal grain diets. Fat in the form of vegetable oil or rice bran can be top-dressed onto the standard grain diet. The upper limit of vegetable oil inclusion seems to be dictated by individual yearling taste preferences and could reach as much as 12 ounces per day.

Something like beet pulp or similar fed after soaking in warm water. The amount fed varies from yearling to yearling, but it is nearly as safe to feed as hay. If the larger amounts of feed are necessary, the daily amount of feed should be split into at least three feedings.

Feeding yearlings excessive amounts of feed in an effort to produce weight gain can lead to a multitude of growth problems along with either colic or laminitis. Sometimes it is best to simply give the yearling some time and let it grow at a slower and safer rate.

Prepping for halter does NOT mean feed that sucker until he's the size of a house on spindly legs! Let your eyes do the talking. If you find this difficult to do maybe you shouldn't be prepping a young horse for the show pen. There is that fine line between fit and fat. **Be careful**.

Always keep monitoring the condition of the horse, as they get older and bigger, feed accordingly. For overweight yearlings, the amount of grain required is less. Often these horses get so little grain that a conventional grain cannot provide adequate nutrient intake. Feeding these individual's a supplement pellet at a reduced rate of just under a kg (1 – 2 pounds) per yearling per day will ensure proper diet fortification.

Keep your eyes on their knees making sure they are not changing in shape and keeping an eye on the growth plates (look at the gap in their knees). Run your hand over this area, hold your hand on the knee for a minute or two to check for heat. Most times if feed or work is overdone you will notice one or both knees developing a bony point on the inside top of their knee…this is not normal.

Young horses, if grown out too quickly or overfed and overworked can develop Epiphysitis

What is Epiphysitis?

Epiphysitis is a condition involving rapid growth of the bone structure in young horses. Often referred to as *compressional physitis*, it may result in growth defects and cause pain. The condition is closely related to contracted tendons.

Affected foals are usually taller than their herd mates or may be foals that are maturing very quickly because of high protein feed. Epiphysitis is the result of rapid bone growth that results in inflammation and swellings on the inside of the fetlock and knee joint. This inflammation of the epiphysical cartilage plate of the long bones usually occurs in the front legs and is caused by excessive pressure from too much weight or too much concussive force on the undeveloped skeletal structure.

The exercise and grooming protocols are similar to those techniques utilized for weanlings. Since yearlings are more mature than weanlings, fewer skeletal wrecks are incurred in an exercise program.

Care should be taken with any exercise program since yearlings are still immature and growing with a real potential for exercise stress injuries. Just as overfeeding the thin yearling can lead to

47

serious problems, overexercising a fat yearling can also lead to serious problems.

Preparing Mature Horses for halter

Preparing mature halter horses for show is significantly easier than either weanlings or yearlings. Mature horses have finished growing and therefore do not experience growth problems as a result of the preparation process. In addition, their bones are mature and can withstand the implications of many different exercise programs.

A Cool Rockstar – Handler Scott Kennedy

Nutritionally, feeding mature halter horses is a task of providing the proper number of calories in the diet to achieve the desired body condition. With the use of high-quality hay and grain, nutrient imbalance with respect to protein, calcium, phosphorus, copper and zinc are unlikely, but if in doubt refer to the section on 'Keeping Your Horse in Tip-Top Health'.

Mature halter horses, like other horses, will have varying rates of metabolism. Therefore, feeding each horse as an individual is essential.

Overfeeding can result in colic and/or laminitis, while underfeeding can result in a thin, non-competitive horse. There are many additional "tricks of the trade" that can be applied to help the halter horse reach his optimum potential, but the successful basics remain the same. It is essential for halter horses -

1.   To be on a properly balanced diet.

2.   Exercise must be carefully designed for each individual animal to avoid potential injury and build the valuable muscle tone that can make a difference between winning and being just another horse in the class.

Careful attention should be paid to daily grooming. There is no substitute for old-fashioned elbow grease. A very valuable characteristic of a good "prepper" is patience. Not every horse will respond as quickly as others and modifications and delays in the process.

Showmanship

Training for showmanship is quite similar to prepping your halter horse in many ways, except for the part where the "Showmanship" class will be judged strictly on the exhibitor's ability to fit and show a horse at halter. The horse is merely a prop to demonstrate the ability and preparation of the exhibitor. The ideal showmanship performance consists of a poised, confident, neatly attired exhibitor leading a well-groomed and conditioned horse that quickly and efficiently performs the requested pattern with promptness, smoothness, and precision. (AQHA 2018).

There are some basic manoeuvres that your horse should know and they are similar to the halter classes however, as mentioned above, *"the class will be judged strictly on the exhibitor's ability to fit and show a horse at halter"*. These are:

- Walk;
- stop;
- jog/trot;
- set-up;
- back-up;
- Pivot.

Other manoeuvres such as 180 degree turns with various combinations of turns or even multiple of these turns.

When teaching your horse at home, it's a good idea to use a halter with the lead chain attached so that when you get to the show your horse is fully acceptable of the chain. If you choose to use a chain, typically, 15 to 20 inches is satisfactory. You don't want more than

10 to 15 inches of chain or lead between your hand and the horse. Don't yank or jerk on the chain – don't expect the chain to make up for lack of training if you decide to use one. Run the chain through the halter starting at the lower, near-side ring, from there, you can run the chain over the horse's nose or under their chin. Run the chain through the off-side lower ring of the halter taking it up to the ring on the side of your horse's cheek making sure you have the snap-lock facing to the outside of the ring ensuring that it won't be rubbed open with the movement of the horse and it is also much safer for you if you need to get it undone in a hurry.

When under the eye of the judge, you should be displaying excellent communication between you and your horse. Present yourself as being confident, walk tall and relaxed. These traits are what the judge will be looking for along with the quality of how your horse will perform the pattern – this is also very important to get right. Do your pattern correctly with smoothness and a lot of quality. Remember, this is a scored class and you should strive to increase your score in the way you present yourself your horse and how you manoeuvre the pattern.

The Walk

Just as you teach your halter horse to walk beside you, it is the same if not *more* important that you train him to walk beside you in the showmanship class not half an inch in front of your shoulder. Keep your horse's throatlatch at your shoulder at all times.

Beginning at the standstill I will use my body language as I did when teaching the young horse for halter prep. I will exaggerate a lean forward in my upper body (my shoulders) which will let my horse know that we are going to walk off, I will also gently pull the lead forward. Try and get your horse to take the first step forward then when you take your step forward you can get in unison with him, both your horse's stride and yours are in mirror fashion. Remember, repetition! The more you halt and repeat the exaggerated shoulder coming forward the quicker your horse will learn to watch your body language. After a while you will no longer need to bring the lead forward, your horse should start to respond to your shoulder tilting forward. Doing this exercise repetitiously will have your horse walking at your side. You will find as you slowly start softening your exaggerated lean forward that you will be able to cue your horse using the slightest tilt forward that only you and your horse will know you are doing it. With repetition this move will be virtually invisible even to the judge and spectators. Do you see how important repetition is now?

Stop

For those of you that are around the same age as me will remember how Yosemite Sam on The Bugs Bunny Show would get off his camel and belt him across the head when he wouldn't stop when asked. He would give him a few whacks and then say "When I say woah, I means whoa!" It was funny at the time, even now it makes me laugh but I suppose it is politically incorrect these days.

When I say whoa,

We do not want to have to stop our horse's in the same way old Yosemite Sam used to that's for sure but when I say whoa, I means whoa! Just as your cues should be invisible, so should your voice commands be silent. So how then do you get your horse to stop?... Body language of course!

When I am about to stop my horse, I will gently pull downward on my lead, use my shoulders again but this time I tilt back rather than forward and at precisely the same time I will say whoa. Make sure you stop dead by planting your feet into the dirt. Then, just as you would in the class when you have acknowledged with the judge that you may now set your horse up for inspection, turn to face your horse with your toes pointing toward your horse's front feet. Once you have done this, turn back facing the front with your horse's throatlatch at your shoulder, lean your shoulders forward to move off as a reminder. Keep repeating this to help your horse understand your body language. When you feel he has got it, cut out the pull-down on the lead, say whoa, lean shoulders back and plant your feet. Eventually you will stop with the verbal "whoa", smooth out the shoulder tilt. In no time with repetition he will begin to stop when you stop, again, you can make the shoulder tilt so subtle that no one will notice it. You will always use the shoulder cue, however, it has to be subtle.

Just as I do when I am in the saddle coming back to the stable at a slow walk, the pace I would walk in the show pen, I do the same when leading a horse whether I'm thinking showmanship or not, the horse has to walk at my shoulder and not drag me back to the stables. Keep your lesson going all the way back to the stable.

Trot

Before I go on to the trot, I like to make sure that my horse has passed with flying colours with the walk lesson. I will always break up my lessons into bite sized pieces before I join it all together as one. Just like those footballers I spoke about, they don't play the actual game until game day comes around.

I will keep this short and sweet because all the cues for the trot are the same as for the walk. The only difference is I will do a soft, single cluck when I am ready for the horse to trot off. The same applies to stopping the horse at the trot as to the walk. Then, when I know the horse has it down pat, I make the shoulder cue very subtle. I keep the single cluck or, if you have to a slow-motion cluck. If you were to stop clucking when you do get in the class, your horse is not a mind reader, you have to let him know you want him to either walk on or trot on, remember all the cues are the same but for the cluck.

Note: When you are executing the trot, it is the same as if your horse was "under saddle", don't let him take two or three walk strides in either the upward transition or the downward transition. When you cue for the jog he must trot off from the get-go or come back down from the trot to the stop, he should not have any walk steps in there.

Note: When trotting off from the judge remember to look ahead, don't look back at your horse or at the judge.

Setup

When setting your horse up it should always be done around the horse's pivot foot – (the right hind). While facing your horse, ask him to stop with his right hind slightly further behind his left hind. With your right hand, pull your horse forward to move his left hind then push back on the lead so that you get him to move his left hind back. Repeat these movements until you have him soft and responsive on moving just the left hind back and forth. Next, you give that a bit of polish by getting him to move his left hind and place it beside his right hind. You need to repeat walking, stopping, turning and pointing your toes in the direction of his right hind, pulling the lead slightly forward with your right hand only, pushing back on the lead with your right hand only. If you do this repetitively, your horse will begin to square up his back legs when you turn to face him. Begin on his front legs, if you have followed how to set up the weanling you will see that it is the same. Do not get your horse used to your toe tapping his hoof when you want him to set his front feet. You can't touch them in the show pen so you may as well get used to it when teaching him to set his front feet at home. Use your lead initially to get them front feet squared.

Back-up

Just as the back-up in a pleasure class can determine a winning or losing run, so it is for showmanship. The judge will be looking for a good level top line and a horse that will back freely with no pressure from the lead. He will also be watching for a straight back up with no veering to the left or the right.

As with the halter horse, I like to train them near a wall or safe fence. I make sure that my body is dead square looking back down the length of the fence and more-so, square on to my horse. If my body is even slightly off kilter my horse will back away from my angle. Picture backing your trailer, if you go right hand down on your steering wheel, the back end of your trailer is going to go left, it's the same with your horse, if you turn and face your horse and your body is angled facing right, even slightly, your horses back end is going to move left when you put pressure on the lead to cue back. When you begin to back your horse using your right hand on the lead, as you put pressure on the lead, keep it central, keep it straight down the main line. Make sure your shoulders are squared and you are walking toward your horse straight. As you keep practicing this, you can again lighten up on the lead, your horse will learn to back-up when you begin to step toward him. The fence will ensure that he is backing straight.

Pivot

Many people have trouble with the pivot. The reason for this is they tend to want to push the horse backwards when indeed it is a forward motion. Another mistake when teaching the pivot is to attempt a full 360 degree turn from the get-go. Like anything you teach your horse, it has to be broken down into parts so that it makes sense to them. First thing you should double check on is that your horse is as straight as a dye from his nose to his tail, points are deducted for a crooked horse.

Facing your horse's neck and with your left hand on the lead, direct your horse to move away from you by pulling slightly forward and to the left, initially you may need to put a bit of knuckle or thumb pressure on his shoulder with your right hand to get him to move away. Take a step toward your horse's front feet. If your horse goes to cross his left front leg behind his right front, you may need to pull him forward more and discontinue to pull the lead toward the left, pull it forward only. Once your horse can cross his left front over his right front and he is responding to your thumb and pull on the lead when doing two to three steps correctly, start to think about the back legs. I don't try for perfection with the front and back legs together, I find it is much easier to break it up by working on the front for correctness first, once they have it then I will begin looking at the back end.

Note: Use your thumb or your knuckles with a push/release movement, don't leave them dug into his shoulder, he will begin to push into the pressure of your thumb or knuckles. It's just like your spur when riding, you don't leave the spurs dug into your horse's sides continually, otherwise they will get dull to the pressure and start ignoring the cue.

Keeping your horse's right hind planted, do the same as you were doing to move the front left over the front right. If your horse wants to place his left hind behind his right hind, remove your thumb pressure and pull him a little forward. Remember to keep his right hind planted. Do a couple of steps and stop, go again, get another couple of steps. In no time at all you can blend all of those few steps so that your horse will be doing a full 360. Start slow and steady and build gradually to the 360. When your horse gets to know these manoeuvres and is doing them on a soft pull with your left hand, swap over to your right hand and keep teaching your horse the moves with the correct hand which is, of course the right hand. You should be able to guide your horse around in the pivot with minimal push.

Showmanship is more about teaching your horse with your body language not with pressure from your hand on the lead. Yes, you start off your training with definite pressure in the directions you wish your horse to go but with repetition your horse will learn to do the manoeuvres on a soft lead rein. You have to be strict on yourself, these exercises need to be worked on daily for at least 20 minutes and at least two to three weeks before you can blend all of your manoeuvres together and begin to finesse for a real pattern. Keep your pattern training to a minimum, you don't want to bore your horse with the same old pattern every day. Working on your speed rather than your accuracy is when a pattern comes in handy. But remember, don't sacrifice your correctness for speed, its brilliant to have both correctness and speed but be patient and build on the speed side of it.

Don't forget to work on your quarter method so that you can make it as smooth and correct as possible, have a friend be your judge, they can walk around your horse while you work on the quarter method.

The exhibitor has to set up the horse and the judge will walk around the animal, as if it were being judged for **conformation**. However, the judge is actually watching the exhibitor and evaluating the grooming, cleanliness, style and turnout of the entry. The exhibitor must move from one side of the horse to the other so that they do not interfere with the judge's line of sight, yet the horse must stand perfectly still, alert, with its ears pricked forward even when the exhibitor moves around. The handler must be particularly smooth and quiet when moving from one side of the horse to the other, yet move quickly and watch the judge at all times.

There are two standard styles used by exhibitors to stay out of the judge's way: the "half system" and the "quarter system." The half system is the simplest, used by beginning exhibitors at small shows, and handy for the halter classes. Though technically legal even for most handlers. In the half system, the handler simply remains on the side (the "half") of the horse opposite that of the judge; when the judge is looking at the left side of the horse, the handler stands on the right, and vice versa.

The quarter system is a bit more complex and is a requirement for showmanship at halter. In the quarter system, the handler stands on the side opposite the judge when the judge is looking at the front of the horse, but when the judge moves to look at the hindquarters of the horse, the handler then moves to stand on the same side of the horse as the judge. The reasoning behind this method is that it is a bit safer in case the horse is startled by the judge being behind it, and it is also easier for the exhibitor to see the judge.

- When the judge is in quadrant I, the exhibitor should be in quadrant IV.
- When the judge moves to quadrant II, the exhibitor should move to quadrant I.
- When the judge moves to quadrant III, the exhibitor should move to quadrant IV.
- When the judge moves to quadrant IV, the exhibitor should move to quadrant I.

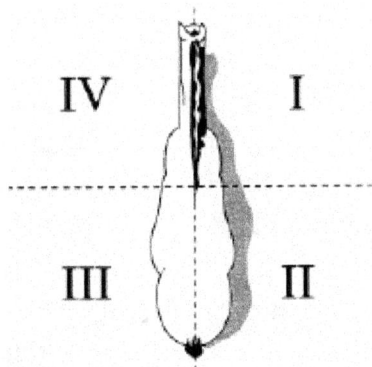

Do you need a round pen?

I like to think of my round pen as a classroom and a 'think tank' rather than as a place to burn off excess energy. I am not a fan of 'free lunging' a horse whether it be in a round pen or out in an arena. I use a round pen with a specific goal in mind. I won't use the round pen to simply burn off energy although, sometimes that can be a real blessing with some horses. The round pen is a great place to start a young horse, it helps to develop control and helps keep all parties safe.

Because the horse is in a round pen doesn't mean that he should be turned out loose in it and allowed to tear around until he runs out of puff. When lunging, I like to make sure I have full control of my horse's speed and how he uses his body.

If you don't have the luxury of a round pen (round-yard), you can lunge your horse on a lunge-lead in your arena or a paddock with a good, flat, safe surface. However, a round pen is a great way to develop body language skills.

If you haven't got a round pen but are in the process of buying a portable round pen or having one built, please, for your horse's sake make sure it is big enough. I realise sometimes it comes down to the mighty dollar that you might need to cut down on the size of your plans to have a decent sized round pen.

The old saying rings true…

You get what you pay for!

What you end up forking money out on is endless vet bills.

Round pen size

A 50-foot (15.24 m) enclosure works well for lunging a horse, but if you plan to ride and train your horse in the pen, you may want to build a round pen with 60 feet (18.28 m) to 80-foot (24.38 m) diameter. My round pen is 60 feet (18.28 m) and works well for lunging, ground driving and riding. I nick named my round pen "The Think Tank" because it truly is a think tank for them. The most common round pen size is 60 feet in diameter. But you can create a pen that is anywhere from 40 to 120 feet in diameter, depending on how much room you would like for you and your horse.

If you are thinking of building your own round pen, you can put the posts in on a slight angle for even more room for the rider. If the posts are set upright you have more chance of having your leg bang into the posts. The pen feels so much roomier when riding if you set the posts on a slight angle, the riders' outside leg hangs freely down beside the horse's body well clear of the posts.

Posts are at a slight angle

What to use for footing?

Filling your pen with ideal footing that is soft enough to absorb the shock and impact of a hoof, but firm enough to support the hoof without overextending the heel or causing toe damage. The footing should drain well, with an approximate 1% slope in the base material. The base should be a flat, contain well-compacted aggregate no larger than ¼", as larger stones can bruise a hoof. The top layer should be four to six inches deep and should retain enough moisture to not be dusty.

Knowing how to use your body language while lunging

As far as I'm concerned, my body language begins as I walk into the barn to start my morning with the horses.

My body language is important when I am around horse's whether I am collecting the horse from the barn to turn them out for the day or to when I am in the saddle. To me, my body language emulates my position with the horse. If I were to be meek and mild, showing signs of uncertainty, horses can read this, they will make the decision that they are the Alpha in this herd.

Because people rely so much on verbal communication, it's natural to focus on a horse's vocalizations when trying to figure out what he is saying. But like many animals, horses communicate much more through postures, gestures and expressions than they do with their vocal cords. So, it makes sense that the horse is picking up on our body language.

Anyone who spends time around horses can learn to use body language to tune in to their nonverbal communication. Better understanding of the language of horses will improve your horsemanship skills, and you'll be able to read your horse more clearly and fine-tune your training and handling accordingly, it all starts with body language

Lunging in the round pen – or the paddock

Horse's can stop reacting to body language because the handler isn't aware of his own body language. For instance, the handler wants the horse to continue to trot, but instead the horse breaks down to a walk because the handler does not realise that he might be looking down or he is not using an open and energetic body language, he uses a slowing body language (for instance, the handler moves his body backwards). Because of this passive body language, the horse starts to walk. The handler then goes to the lunge whip and begins to hunt the horse on with his whip. Soon enough, the horse learns to ignore the handler's body language. The horse will now only respond to pull on the lunge lead or the lunge whip.

Where you are standing in relation to your horse when lunging will be part of how you converse with your horse. From the time you send your horse off into a larger circle your body language needs to be in a "driving" position, you will be telling your horse to move off away from you. It's not always necessary to use a lunge whip to get your horse moving off. That's not to say you can't use a whip however, you want to be able to check with your horse how much "push" you need to use. You don't want to start at the strongest end of the push, check first, you may be able to move your horse off with less push than you think especially if you are using your correct body language which in the long run will be in your favour if you are going to be lunge lining your yearling.

A Neutral body language will be what you use when you are happy with how your horse is travelling, many handlers make the mistake of pushing the horse on continually, this too, will have your horse ignoring your cues. You have to 'give' and 'take'.

A Driving body language is positioning yourself to being opposite the flank or hind quarters, you are now allowing the horse to move ahead of you a little. You are now 'behind' the horse and, therefore, able to encourage him forward more effectively. When in this position, have your body position facing the head of your horse not facing his flank – stand opposite the flank – position your body so that you are looking at his face. Keep your body 'open', have your lead hand out away from your side as if you are pointing in the direction you want your horse to travel, your other arm should also be out away from your body and on an angle that is facing your horse's hip. This is a driving body position. You can have a lunge whip in your hand as an extension of your arm for a little more encouragement. Kiss to your horse while in this open position, if you take a purposeful step toward your horse this will also encourage him to move up into the lope. Coming back to the 'neutral' position will slow your horse down, bringing him back to the jog or walk.

Equally as important is your ability to 'steady' your horse going forwards. If your horse is travelling way too fast at the canter, position yourself slightly forward of your horse's shoulder, position your lead arm in a way that it is now pointing slightly in front of his nose, using your voice cues steady your horse with a calming voice, turning your torso so that you are facing his shoulder or just behind.

Don't forget about *your* legs, think about *your* speed, it's easy to get sucked in to emulating your horse's stride, If the horse is taking short, quick strides, I will slow my legs down, I'll take longer, slower strides. I want the horse to begin to relax and emulate my long, slow strides. I may not see any change in this horse's movement for days, I just keep on keeping on, lengthening and slowing my stride. I know the horse will eventually follow my rhythm. It's the same in the saddle, if the horse takes shorter strides, I slow my seat down, change the rhythm and stick with it, the horse will come back to me. Some smaller horse's (not all) may not have a lot of "ground time" where they tend not to hold the ground for very long and "air time", I can tweak the ground and air time a little by slowing my seat, ride in a slow rhythm with steady hands. When he sucks back and relaxes into my rhythm it will show in his expression that he is relaxed, he will look through the bridle. I won't try and force a round peg into a square hole. If I show this particular horse with a bit of "showmanship" on my part, showing him on a loose rein, he is looking through the bridle, has a good top line, a nice expression, rounded and driving from behind, he is doing the job to the best of his ability, I can't ask for more than that. I won't stress too much about his shorter ground and air time. Getting hot under the collar about something you can't change too much will see you getting shown the gate.

Teaching your yearling to lunge

Doll's Got Style

When starting out with your yearling teaching them to lunge, I like to start out by taking them into the round yard. This makes it a bit more controlling for the first couple of weeks to "explain" to your horse the principle of lunging.

At this stage, the lead is clipped underneath the jaw on the ring, I don't want to use a lot of pressure initially. I believe you should always start at the bottom end of the pressure dial and if needed, work your way up until you find the "goldilocks" pressure for that particular horse.

Just before they graduate to being lunged outside of the round pen it is then that I change where I clip the lead.

I like to wait until they are moving out, slowing down, stopping quite well and they are listening and watching my cues then I will place a rope underneath the jaw of a young one or short chain.

Fastening the rope or chain through the noseband of the yearling's halter...

      1. Starting at the underside bottom ring slide up through the near-side ring;
      2. Run the rope/chain over the front of the halter;
      3. Place it through the off-side ring of the halter;
      4. Bring back to the underside bottom ring.

NOTE: *If this is too severe on your yearling, clip it onto the lunge line ring (back to itself). This is "Dead Ring" meaning it won't tighten or loosen. Don't have too much chain, lock it back to itself, this will take up the slack.*

Definitely NOT recommended using a chain on a young baby.

Colts that are a bit headstrong I will switch it out for a chain. I like to keep the chain on the shorter side, if it is too long it may swing and hurt them or they will become afraid of it making them move away rather than to it.

Further along in their training I like to use a flat nosed leather side-pull, (see the one below) they are softer on their nose area than a rolled rawhide noseband but are still one up on a plain nylon or leather halter.

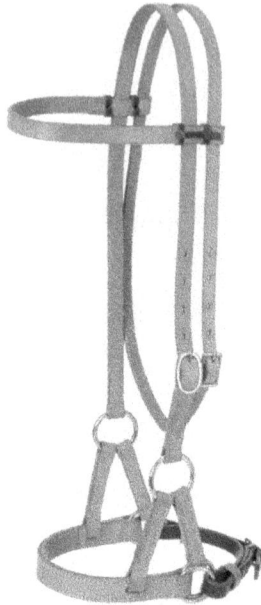

Leather Flat Nosed Side-Pull

However, I won't start using the side-pull until they are completely trained and familiar and comfortable with everything that is being done with them. Another bonus with using the side-pull is that they are used to the feel of it when they are being broken in for riding.

Five positive points to using a rope/chain under the jaw

1. Differentiates between being led around to getting worked
2. Aids in finessing the frame and how they carry themselves
3. Helps keep them from dropping their inside shoulder
4. Softens the cues up
5. Give you more control

Hold the lunge line properly

You may instinctively think that wrapping the lunge line around your hand or wrist will help you maintain a better grip, but such a hold is actually quite dangerous. If the horse panics and takes off, you would be dragged along with it or have your hand or fingers broken by the quickly tightening rope. Instead, it's best to hold the line in such a way that you can maintain control but still let go if necessary. This isn't much of a problem in a confined area like a round pen, however, it's going to be a little different when you move out into the open. Fold the lunge line back and forth to create a stack of folded line.

Feed the line out from the top of your folded line stack and attach that end to your horse.

Hold the line in the centre of the stack and let additional line out as needed. If your horse panics for any reason, let go of the line so you are not dragged.

I also like to use a lunge rope that has been weighted at the horse end of the rope. I wouldn't recommend using a weighted rope every single time you train them. Switch your ropes up now and again to help keep them light in hand.

Position yourself in the circle

Stand in the circle with the lunge line stacked into a folded line and held in one hand. You'll want to stand at the horse's side facing its shoulder. Hold the lead with your hand approximately 2 to 4 inches (5 to 10 centimetres) from the snap. Using your right hand holding the whip (I prefer not to use a whip in the show pen, I like to raise my right arm up and out away from my body for the cue to move off). Encourage him to move off from you. As he moves away slide your left hand down the line giving him more and more rein.

Use the whip in the early stages

The lunge whip is one of your most important tools in teaching your horse in the early stages of training to move on steadily. Use it as an extension of your arm. Raising it up and clucking to move him out. You can crack the lunge whip now and again to get him to move off. Once your yearling is listening and watching your cues with the whip in hand, try all of your body cues minus the whip.

The lunge whip I feel, is not needed in your training when you begin to finesse his movements. Raising your arm's higher for the lope cue, lower to come back to the jog and dropped down for the walk, at your side and still for whoa. Wait a few seconds, then repeat the whole process until your horse learns to follow your cues.

Be in control of the lunge lesson

Getting a yearling trained up for lunge line is different from lunging them for exercise. Also, we tend to do the same thing every day when we take them out into the round yard for exercising. We tend to let them choose if they want to trot, canter or walk, then we stop them, turn them and do the same thing in the other direction. However, when prepping them for lunge line it pays to keep everything calm and slow motion.

If your yearling is full of himself and just wants to play around, unclip the lead shank and send them off to get a lot of that steam out of them. When they look like they have got all or most of that extra energy out, hook them back up and begin the lesson.

Move away at a walk

Once you have your yearling moving out away from you at a nice pleasurable walk keep them walking for a few circles. If they are going to continue to walk then that's great.

If they want to hoon around on the end of the lead, I will usually make them work for it. If they take off to the left for example shaking their head, kicking out, galloping and they just want to play out there on the end of the line, I will stop them, send them off in the other direction which would be off to the right. If they are still playing around, bucking or pigrooting, I will stop them again and turn them to the left.

This is done as close to one movement as possible. What I mean by that is don't stop them, hesitate while you are gathering your lead rein then ask them to trot off. Its stop-turn-move off all in one move. (Naturally, turning them in toward the inside of the circle).

This is going to get the sting out of them a lot quicker than anything else especially if they want to play around for a few revolutions.

They don't seem to want to keep up this façade when it is you that is in charge, it's no longer their idea to go mental and play around. Suddenly they realise that you are actually making them work, they won't want to keep going for long when they realise it's no longer a game.

Always keep them guessing

Always remember that you are *training* them for lunge line *not* doing the routine of the movements when you are at home.

An example is with footballers, every night through the week they go to football practice, they will practice all of their moves, tackles, kicks etc but they won't actually play a game of football and that is exactly what you want to do with your yearling.

Try not to get out there and walk for one and a half circles, jog the same and lope then back to a walk and then halt and repeat in the other direction. Mix it up at home, keep them second guessing what is coming next otherwise you will fall short in the show pen when your yearling knows it is time to jog or its time to stop and reverse. Keep them on their toes when it comes to what is coming up next. You might walk a few circles, reverse and walk on today. Tomorrow you might walk five circles then ask for the jog, then walk on. Just mix it up every day. When you get closer to show day that's when you can polish it up a bit and work on the actual routine as if you were under the eye of the judge.

Sweating the neck

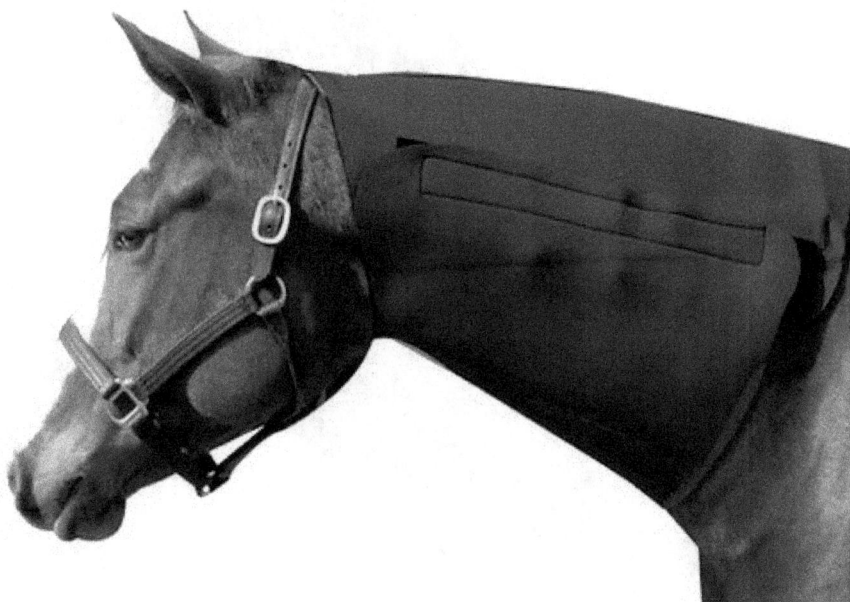

Neoprene Neck Horse Sweat, Black

If you think that your yearling could do with a little lightening off through the neck it's a good idea to invest in a neoprene neck sweat.

I would recommend also a neoprene Jowell sweat. Put this on first then put the full neck sweat over the top. You can even put some Glad Wrap around their necks first then put the neoprene sweats over the top.

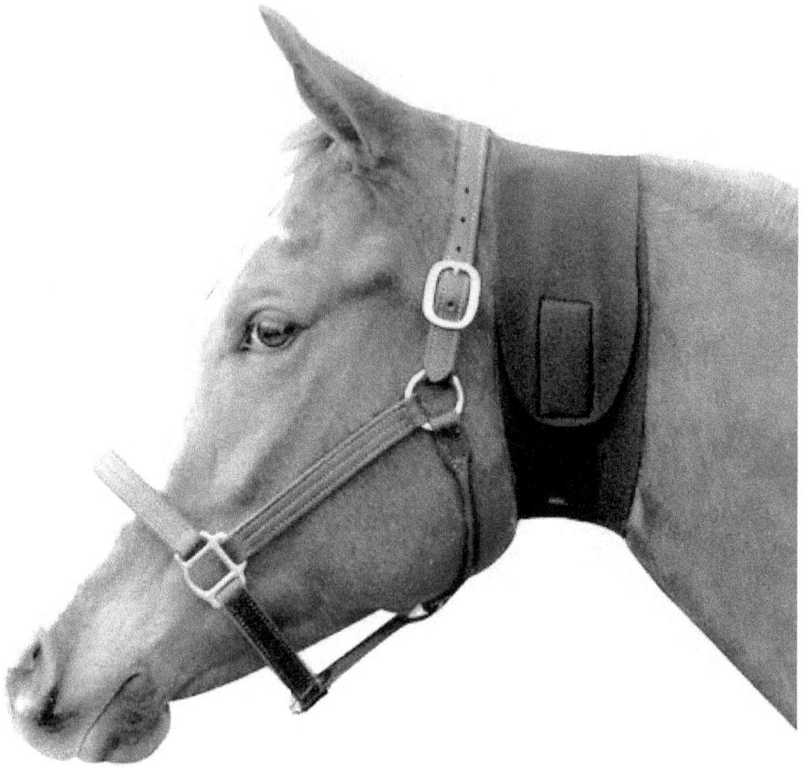

Neoprene Jowl Sweat, 10-Inch, Black

Because you're not really out there in the round pen for speed and sweat, put the sweats on when you feed up in the morning, tie them up at the feed bin (if it is attached to the wall, don't tie them if their feed bin is on the ground especially if you are going to disappear for a cup of coffee while they are eating. You could wait until they have finished eating, bring them out of their stable and tie them up with the sweats on in the sunshine and let nature do the work for you while you clean their stable out.

Work your horse with the neck sweats on then when you have finished working with them in the round pen, tie them up again with the sweats intact for up to 45 minutes to an hour afterward. Hopefully it's not a freezing cold day – you won't get much sweat out of them in the cold.

Boot up – ALWAYS!

Never forget to place splint boots ESPECIALLY on the front legs of your yearling, or wrap them. If you can it's also not a bad idea to either wrap their back legs or put on some back boots for protection. Remember, they are in their prime of growing, having growth spurts, they still have gaps in their knees. They really do need their legs protected.

Transitioning to an arena

Around about 60 days of teaching your yearling the ins and outs of lunging in a round pen It's now time to get them out in the arena or an open space.

Yearling Lunge-Line competition is not done in a round yard so we have to get them out in the open and teach them the ropes without a secure barrier holding them in.

- Start them from the centre of your circle. Always start at a walk.
- When they first come out read their energy levels, if they're full of beans let them work it out before you start the training session with them.
- Don't automatically look for a slow jog too early. Bring them back down and ask again. Similar to how I explained in the round pen when they wanted to play around only this time bring them back and ask again until they give you what you are asking for.
- If they want to canter off – let them but let them know it was your idea so push them on for 3 or 4 rounds, make them canter.

The closer in they are to you the more comfortable they are. Don't think in the mindset that you have to have them at show length of 30 feet. That comes later on when they get flatter and slower, once that happens you can put them out further on the lead naturally.

Reverse

This is the same as the stop. It's an important part of the training. By nature, they're going to turn in on you because you're pulling on the rope so this is where the verbal cues are used.

When you ask them to stop ask them several times then pull on the rope and wait.

When you go to reverse, pull them into that direction with body language. Encourage them to move away. You may need to lift your arms to show them you want them away from you.

Here, if they want to trot off just shorten your lead, bring them in closer, verbally cue them to slow to the walk. Keep bringing them closer until you get a nice, flat footed walk.

Don't leave them there too long at the walk. It's still early in their training and that's a lot of attention span for a baby.

If your horse gets to moving too quickly and out of control, bring them in closer. Then encourage them back to the gait that you wanted.

When stopping them, don't turn them around every time or they will stop listening to your cue, they will begin to automatically stop and turn around – always keep them guessing.

Be sure that you are behind their eye, if you get in front of their eye you will be asking them to stop because you will be blocking their forward motion.

These are all the basic things I do with them for about 30 to 60 days. I am not looking for them to have all the gaits perfect at this point. It's just getting them conditioned to the distance of the rope, the pressure of the chain or the rope around their noseband and getting them used to your cues both with your body language and verbal.

I am not too concerned at this point either if they lope off on the wrong lead, all of these things will fall into place with more experience. If they do take the wrong lead don't reprimand them for it just shorten the lead line, drop them back down to a trot and ask again.

Stopping

End result – you don't want them turning in on you when you want them to stop but, in the beginning, you are going to have to be pulling on the lead to get them to understand they have to stop. Try several times to use the verbal cue "whoa" so you don't encourage them to turn in.

Intermediate Lunge Line Training

Now that your horse is more in-tune with your cues, he has slowed his gaits down and is listening and waiting on your cues, dependant on the type of nature your horse has you need only bring them out 3 days a week to practice your speeds, cues, length of the line etc. If you have one that is laid back and easy going you really don't need to be drilling them every day, this would just have them anticipating everything and becoming sour. The more energetic type of horse that is less inclined to want to slow into the gaits or to listen to you then you would be bringing them out every day and working on the cues etc.

Starting them off in the centre of the arena again, have them walk away from you in a nice, flat footed walk. This is a time where you can get a feel of what their energy levels are that day, if they are full of beans and excited don't leave them at the walk for too long, cue them up to a trot, let them get some energy out of them before you begin your lunge line training.

If, on the other hand, your horse is docile in nature and willing to go slow, push them up into a trot also, if you have them in the lope, push them up into a canter. If you let them go in "show speed" all of the time they will start to become and look lazy, dragging their toes, dropping their shoulder and just going through the motions.

Don't **Show** them – **Train** them.

Once you know your horse is seasoned to show, make sure you don't practice the show routine because they will begin anticipating what you're going to do. If your horse has a great break-down from the lope to the jog or they have a real pretty stop, don't keep doing it over and over. Number 1. They will anticipate it and Number 2. It can be hard on their legs and joints when overdone. When they are at this stage of training you need to keep them fresh, happy and learning. Do lots of extensions in your gaits in order to keep the shortening of strides out.

Once you are happy with how they are moving out, let them slow to show speed for a moment then move them back out again keeping their minds fresh.

Encourage them to move out on the line, using up the full length of the line by opening up your body by lifting and opening your arms and moving toward them. Walk with them as well as toward them. This will get them moving out onto the end of the line. You can have a voice command like 'out' or 'move' whatever you like to get them out to the end of the line. Kiss them up into the lope, again, asking for a bit more extension than what they would do in the show pen.

To get your horse to pick up their pace, you have to pick up your pace, to slow them down you have to show them that you have slowed down. Standing still will help you stop them, along with your voice cues. When you ask them for the whoa, don't let them come in, make them stop facing the direction they are going in.

When stopping and turning, if your line is loose and dragging on the ground, you know that they are not quite straight, they are turning in slightly, they haven't completed a full 180 degree turn. You need to walk a step or two toward them with open body language and your chosen voice cue, they may step out really quickly and want to keep moving on so be ready to say whoa, get them to halt for a bit before continuing on. Make sure they stop straight.

Once you get them walking on if they start caving in on you again, repeat your body language and walk toward them until they move out. Don't let them jog until they are settled and staying on a full line.

Verbal Tones, Body Language and Feel a day keeps the lunge whip away

When using your verbal cues make sure they can differentiate between a reprimand and a reward tone. They need to know if what they are doing is good or bad. They like a bit of praise so don't just use your angry tones.

Make sure you repeatedly use the same body language you have developed every time you train your horse so that he gets to know what each cue means. When you want your horse to speed up or extend the gait be sure to shorten the line a bit so that they can 'feel' something is coming that they need to do. Open up your body language.

This is how you can get by without using a whip. Train them to read your cues and understand them – you won't need a lunge whip.

Exit and Entry Gate

It's a very good idea to sometimes train them at your exit/entry gate. It's a really good time to smooth out any bad habits they may have of trying to get to the gate. Give them the opportunity at home before you go out to a show to make the mistake of trying to leave then you can work on it at home.

Problems in Certain Areas

If your horse is having a problem at a certain point of his circle, he may have spotted your neighbour working in his garden or spotted an object that wasn't there yesterday. Instead to loping around and around waiting for them to forget about whatever is spooking them. Take them back to the problem area and address the problem.

You might have tried loping them off at a certain spot when they have spooked at 'old mate' next door, they might have run off or run in toward you. Take them back there and work on loping off again. This is an excellent opportunity to work on problems that occur before you take them out.

Know your horse – know your surroundings and conditions

By now you should be getting the feel of how long your horse needs before he is flat footed and listening to you. Some horses may take 20 to 30 minutes before they are ready to work with you, others only 10 minutes before the edge is knocked off. On top of that, be aware of what your horse is like on any given day. What is your horse like to work with on a windy or cold day compared to a hot day?

Lunge Line

The purpose of showing a horse on a lunge line is to demonstrate that the horse has the movement, manners/expression/attitude and conformation to become competitive under saddle.

This class defines what it means to be a Western Pleasure prospect or Hunter Under Saddle prospect.

Yearlings are not expected to demonstrate the behaviour or quality of a finished show horse, but only that performance necessary for a reasonable presentation to the judge.

Therefore, the purpose of this class is to reward:

- Quality of movement, manners, expression and attitude;
- Conformation suitable to future performance and the horse is to be judged with its suitability as a future performer under saddle in mind. (AQHA 2018)

Now that you have put some hard work in training your yearling in the lunge line, you are ready to go and test the waters at a show. If you are lucky enough to find a local show that has lunge line on their program, it would be a good idea to give your horse his first taste at one of the locals before heading off to one of the major shows. If not, don't let that stop you, I find it is less stressful to treat every show as a local show.

I know in some areas a lot of horse owners that are chewing at the bit so to speak to get their yearlings out as soon as they can, they may not live in an area where they hold many local shows. If this is you, I would recommend taking your yearling to some of the shows that are held, before he is at the correct age to be shown legally as per the rule book, you will be able to show him in his age group halter class there. After he has been shown in his class, you could stay on with him and perhaps work him on the lunge in the lunch break or at least get him to these local shows and hang out with him so that when the big one comes around it will be second nature to him when he arrives.

Class Order

Conformation and Equipment Inspection. – Each horse will be inspected by the judge on conformation and equipment, they will also check for evidence of abuse and inhumane treatment.

When called in by the Ring Steward, you will be required to square your horse up at the entry cones.

Whether you are showing your yearling as a Hunter horse or a Western horse, the squaring up is the same. When given the nod by the judge you will approach the judge at the walk, halt and square up for inspection. You will be asked to show your Mares/fillies and stallions/colts teeth. From this point you will jog/trot (depending on your discipline Hunt or Western) to and around the next cone.

As you walk to and jog/trot from the judge, they will be watching how the horse tracks, they will be watching to see if the horse strikes himself or any interference in any way that would show unsoundness.

Turning left at the cone at the jog/trot, the judge will then be able to see your horse's profile and how well they are stepping out and clearing the ground. The judge will get an overall picture of your horse's top line and movement.

If you are showing your yearling as a hunt horse be sure to trot the horse out, show off his movement. The judge will want to see a nice, ground covering walk stride. At the trot he should have a soft, long, flat footed stride and have a flat top line – show your horse off to the judge to demonstrate his hunter stride. The judge needs to see a difference between a jog and a trot when presenting your lunge liner as a hunt horse.

When presenting your yearling as a hunt horse you can fit him up with a plain leather halter with brass fittings. The lead shank can be brass to match in with the halter. You, the handler, can be dressed in English attire.

If your hunt horse tends to be a little sensitive you can show him with a plain leather lead minus the shank chain, they may be a little worried about the chain so, if you decide to do this, best to train your horse at home with it, don't train at home with the shank then change at the show to a plain lead. Make sure your horse is well behaved and comfortable at home the way you intend to show him.

Having said that, you will not be penalised for using a regular halter, nor are you to be rewarded for using a show halter and show lunge line. For the conformation inspection a lead shank, such as used in halter or showmanship classes, can be exchanged for the lunge line prior to the lunging demonstration.

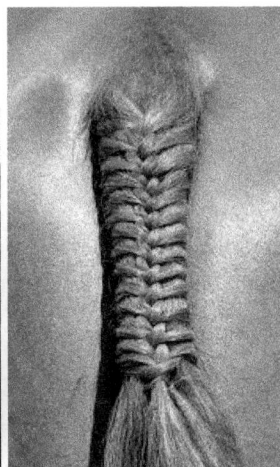

English braid

If you are showing at one of the larger shows, you can braid your horse's mane in an English braid you can even go the whole mile and braid their tail. It's not necessary however, it looks professional, show the judge that you are "in it to win it". Have your horse and yourself well presented.

"Setting" the Western Horse

Setting up with the western horse for conformation inspection is the same as with the hunt horse. It's crucial that you put time and quality into your set up, it's not necessary to work your quarters for the judge in this class like you would with a showmanship class. Once you set your horse up, keep yourself out of the judges view of your horse so that they get a full view of your horse's profile, their front and back end.

"Trainability" is scored just as conformation is scored.

When jogging your horse out for the judge, it should be a definite two beat jog, not a trot as you would with a hunt horse.

Fitting the western horse with a silver halter or regular, be sure to fit it tight in the throat latch to accentuate the horse's head. You can use the shank in the presentation however, it is not allowed when lunge lining the horse. If you prefer, you can exchange the lead shank, such as one used in halter or showmanship classes, for the lunge line prior to the lunging demonstration.

Lunging Demonstration –

The minimum length of the lead is 6 metres, maximum is not to exceed 9 metres. As long as the equipment being used meets the requirements it is not a consideration in placing. The only thing that you should be being judged on is manners, expression, way of going and conformation.

Western attire is mandatory, except if a prospect is considered to be a hunt prospect then conventional English attire will be required.

Once your horse has reached the perimeter of the circle, your time will begin. Once the signal to begin is given, you will have 1 ½ minutes (90 seconds) to present the horse at all three gaits in both directions be it walk, jog, lope or walk, trot, canter.

When "time" is called to commence your workout, walk a ¼ circle at least, jog a full circle then lope. When half time is called you ideally want your horse to stop in a straight line, don't let them turn in to you then stop or walk toward you. Try to get your horse to rotate back on his hocks to turn, walk on ¼ circle, jog full then lope till whistle calls time.

It's pretty important to know your horses timing, zone in on it at home.

If by chance you have a horse that has an excellent jog and his lope is average, I personally would show the jog for a little longer than one lap before putting them up into the lope.

Your horse's manners, expression and attitude will count for up to 10 points of the total score.

Conformation will count for up to 20 points of the total score.

Go for the bonus points

Really think about using your circle because there are bonus points here so you may as well get them.

- +3 = Excellent
- +2 = Good
- +1 = Adequate
- +0 = General

You MUST get your minimum in to be scored. – minimum ¼ walk, ½ jog, if you don't get one full circle at the lope ON the correct lead in the lope you won't be scored higher than any other entry. If your horse breaks gait or cross fires bring him back, lope him off again and go for that full circle on the correct lead. If this happens to you going the first way, you may have to hustle the second way to make your time.

You will be penalised for

- excessive trotting into the lope
- wrong lead
- balking
- obvious signs of overwork
- sourness such as ear pinning
- head throwing
- striking
- tail wringing
- a dull, lethargic way of going
- touching the horse with the whip
- running off
- excessive bucking
- cutting into the circle
- backing up on the lunge
- excessive urging from the exhibitor
- cross firing/cantering

You will be disqualified for

- lameness
- striking horse with whip
- if the horse falls. (all four legs are extended in the same direction)
- horse stepping over or getting tangled in lunge line
- failure to show at all three gaits in both directions
- loss of control of the horse to the point that the horse is loose in the arena

Led Trail

Yearlings and 2-year-olds

This class is judged on the performance of the horse over and through obstacles with emphasis on manners, response to the handler and attitude. Contestants will travel, leading the horse on a halter/lead over or through 6 trail obstacles, to be chosen by the judge and posted minimum of one hour prior to the beginning of the class. The course will consist of any obstacles which could reasonably be expected to be encountered on a trail ride. Credit will be given to horses negotiating the obstacles with style, expression and a degree of speed, providing carefulness is not sacrificed. Special credit is given to a horse picking its way through an obstacle that warrants it and willingly responding to a handler's cues on other obstacles. Horses shall be penalized for any unnecessary delay while approaching or negotiating the obstacles or for blatant disobedience. They will also be penalized for failure to demonstrate correct lead or gait, if designated, failure to complete obstacles, failure to follow correct line of travel within or between obstacles or for performing obstacles incorrectly or other than specified order or no attempt to perform an obstacle.

Desensitizing

Sometimes you come across yearlings that are a little spooky, they want to lean on you and practically try and jump into your arms for protection. The best thing you can do for this type of horse is work with them every day teaching them with lots of patience.

I had one like this, it needed a great deal of work. What I liked to do was keep a big piece of rubber matting on the ground on the way in and out of the stables. Every time I got him out to exercise him, he had to travel across the mat. He was one that nearly *did* jump into my arms a few times.

Patience was the virtue. Daily, I would put an old show halter on him, bring the lead chain right around his nose, not to pull him around and hurt him, to let him know when that chain is on, it's time to work and listen.

He was really worried about walking over the rubber at first. Either walking right behind me about to jump on me or leaning on me the whole time. When he tried leaning on me, I would just move over to his right and hold him still, letting him see what was going on out of his left eye. I would move back to the left side and make him stand. This went on for a few days.

The worst thing I could have done would have been to rush him just to get him to get over the rubber. I just concentrated on getting him on the mat straight and in his own space all along getting him to have confidence in me and trust.

Once I could see that he was fine with stopping and standing on the mat I began bringing him right over. Once over, I would stop him again. I would turn him toward me and continue going back over it, I would then do a few walk overs with a push away from me when I turned him to go back over the rubber. So, he was not only getting used to the scary rubber matting, he was learning the pull toward and the push away, he would definitely see this in the show pen so why not train him while he was working the mat.

When working on this exercise, if your horse puts their head down to look at the mat, this is a good thing, don't reprimand them for this as it is a great trait for them to have in the show pen when they approach logs, bridges etc. to have expression when approaching, try and nurture that if you can.

Also, lead them over the mat from the right-hand side and stop them from the right-hand side. Do as many things as you can like this to help desensitise them.

Poles

When starting your yearling on poles I like to start with one pole only, just walking over it practicing the pull toward and push away turn to go back over the same log.

Once they're good with that, I place a pole to the side of the existing pole making an L shape, I put this over near the arena fence because that is like a blocker if they want to refuse the log the fence is there to give them the feel that they have to go over the log, there is no out.

You can then begin to walk them over the first log then do a push away turn over the side log, push away turn to come back over, this will then be a pull toward turn. You can play around with that whenever you are out in the arena with them.

Jog Poles

Always be stride for stride with your horse, you don't want to be pulling them behind you or, even worse being dragged along.

Once again, I like to start with one pole, jogging one way, stopping, turning and jogging back over the same pole. I will go from one pole to putting at least 10 to 12 poles out in a straight line to start. I will jog them through this straight line of poles totally ignoring the carnage they may create behind us. I will jog on out of the straight line, jog a wide turn (pull toward) and jog back through the poles. If they have made the line of poles look like pick up stick's I will get them back in order however, I don't worry about their spacing, I like to mix the spacing up. I like them to be mindful of where they are about to place their feet, if the poles are mixed up a bit distance wise it encourages them to look at the poles which will give the horse more expression.

From the straight-line poles, I will divide them up and have two poles in one place, four in alongside them, three alongside and another three parallel with the four poles.

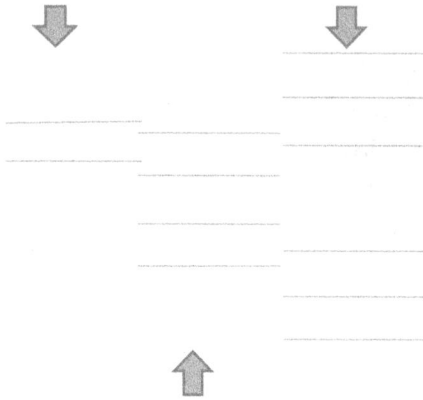

⬇   ⬇

⬆

See the diagram above complete the poles in the direction of the arrows, leaving yourself plenty of jogging room when turning. Go in the direction of the arrows until you feel that they are finding their feet really well underneath them then once again, reverse and go in the other direction which will be a little more difficult as it becomes a push away turn. At this early stage, don't worry too much about them ticking and hitting the poles with their feet, the last thing you want is for them to fear hitting a pole. However, if they tend to be drifting away from you off the poles, the next time around I will go wider to the left to keep them in the middle of the poles. If you have one that gets a bit excited by the momentum of jogging over the poles and wants to speed up when they are going over them, put them in a jog when you come out of the poles but then break them down to a walk when you come back to go over the logs until they settle down then go back to jogging the poles.

The Bridge

I like to start a young horse on ground level before introducing the height of the bridge.

To start off, I make it look interesting and more like a bridge than just stepping over the poles and back onto the flat ground. I will use some drums on the sides of the "make-shift bridge. At the beginning and end of the bridge I place a couple of poles with one end raised up on one and the opposite end of the other pole raised up in a criss-cross shape. You can use a pole before that so that the horse has to step in between the pole and the raised cross.

This method is great for giving them the confidence to see an object and step over the logs into the object before you have them stepping up onto a wooden bridge. It's also great for getting them to look down at the logs, more expression training! Always be sure to have your horse traveling alongside you and not following along behind or dragging you through the obstacles, always do the obstacles both ways so that you can practice your push and pull turns.

KLI She's My Priority

You should always remember you and your horse want to blend with each other and be one unit. To achieve this, you need to keep your movements smooth and calm. If you get to pulling and jerking, it will show up in your horse's movement and expression.

Be sure that you approach all of the obstacles completely straight. I will then introduce them to the raised bridge.

In the early stages of training horses over the bridge, you will get some that jump or slip off the sides of the bridge because they are reluctant to go over it. So, for the first few times of traveling over, I use temporary sides that I can take away really easily. These temporary sides help them stay straight on the bridge.

If at any time the horse spooks and tries to escape the obstacle, stop them and stand for a bit before you bring them back to the obstacle and try again, don't reprimand them at this early stage. If, on the other hand, you have a seasoned horse that is repeatedly doing this kind of thing, I would encourage you to stop them, back them, put them into a couple of 360's, re-group then continue on with your training.

I like to put a lot of variation into my training, it keeps them fresh, no-one likes to do something exactly the same day in, day out so once your horse is going over the raised bridge both ways fairly well, start the push turn at the bottom of the raised bridge and walk them into the make-shift bridge, over the poles and back around to the raised bridge. This is very good not only for practicing your push turn but it stops them from wanting to speed up once they come off that bridge. If you're turning them into the entrance of the make-shift bridge it will stop them from speeding up. The more opportunities you get to get them waiting on you the better so if they want to rush off coming off the bridge, stop and wait.

Led Trail – Side pass

Training a horse to side pass is beneficial for multiple reasons, whether it be improving groundwork, being able to open a gate while seated, or preparing for yearling/two-year-old led trail class. Fortunately, the process of teaching a horse to side pass includes training a turn on the haunch and on the forehand, two other useful groundwork and riding techniques. Follow these steps, and you'll improve not only your riding but your horse's response and performance.

Test your horse's ability to move away from pressure. The natural instinct of your horse should be to move away from where pressure is applied – the same instinct humans have. Test this reaction in your horse by bumping them with an open palm near the girth where you would bump them with your calf. They should move away from your hand, possibly already in a side pass.

- Continue bumping your horse near the girth with added pressure if they do not respond to you. As soon as they take a step away, release pressure and reward them.
- Practice this until your horse needs only a single bump, or no bump at all (just pushing energy with your hand towards their girth), in order to move away from you.

Train a turn on the haunch.

Put your horse on a lead rope, and if necessary, grab a crop. Stand so that your body is positioned slightly behind the barrel of your horse's body, and gesture with your arm or crop towards their shoulder. If they do not respond to this, then apply pressure on their shoulder. The goal is to get them to move away from your pressure by rotating their body around their back legs.

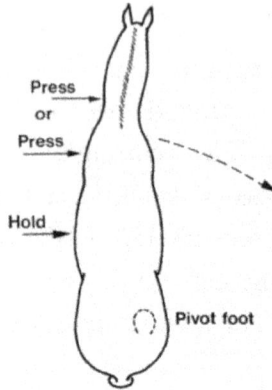

Haunch turn on the right rear pivot foot. It may be necessary to push on the shoulder first.

- If your horse turns away or simply walks in the opposite direction rather than crossing their front legs in a turn, grab the lead rope and hold them straight ahead.
- As soon as your horse crosses their front legs in a turn on the haunch, release pressure and reward them for doing what you asked.
- Continue practicing a turn on the haunch on the ground, your horse will respond to the same cues when riding.

Train a turn on the forehand.

Similar to a turn on the haunch, a turn on the forehand is done when your horse rotates their entire body around their front legs by crossing their back legs. Accomplish this by standing near the shoulder (to block shoulder/forward movement) and gesturing towards the haunch with your crop or open hands. If they don't respond without pressure, add a bit by pushing against the haunch with your open hands, or tapping them with the crop.

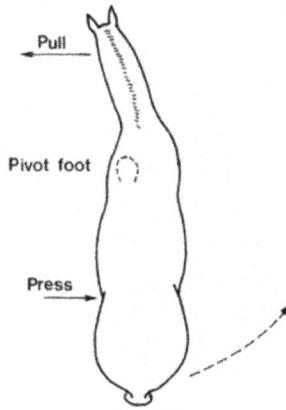

Forehand turn on left front pivot foot.

- Don't remove pressure if your horse simply backs away or turns to the side. Straighten them out if necessary, but continue bumping with pressure until they take at least one step by crossing their legs.
- As soon as your horse achieves a single step in a turn on the forehand, release pressure and reward them for following your cues.
- Practice this over and over until your horse requires a minimal amount of pressure to accomplish a turn on the forehand.

Combine your groundwork to accomplish a grounded side pass.

Stand next to your horse near the barrel of their body, using a crop if necessary. Bump the girth of the horse to tell them to move away; if they don't move how you want, give them the cues for a turn on the haunch and a turn on the forehand. Continue working back and forth between your cues until your horse clues in and does at least a single successful step in a side pass.

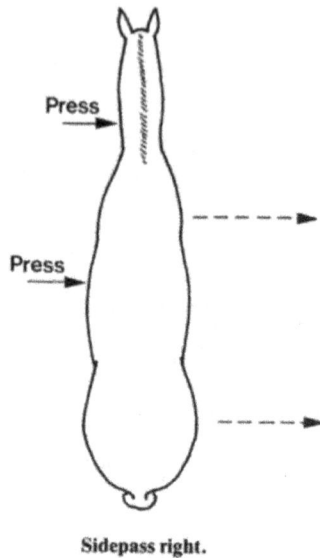

Sidepass right.

- Reward your horse and release pressure as soon as they take even a single step in the form of a side pass.
- Continue doing this until they don't need to be cued for a turn on the forehand and a turn on the haunch in order to recreate a side pass. Eventually they should only need to be bumped on their side near the girth. And if you use clear body language, you will be able to get them to side pass with your cue without touching their bodies.

The Fan

The Fan is an arc turn where you would lay out three to four poles all meeting together in the middle and fanning out – just like a fan!

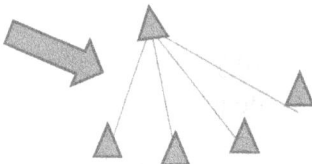

- When doing the fan at the walk, you will naturally want to start in closer to where all the poles meet because you will be going at a shorter stride.
- The jog will vary on the stride and height of your horse. Long striding horses would be taken out further toward the ends of the poles. A shorter striding horse would be better taking the middle of the poles.

The trick is to know your horse's stride. Study them when you are practicing and work out where you might like to tackle this obstacle on your horse's stride.

If your horse is a bit nervous at first about jogging the poles, jog when you are out of the poles and then break them down to a walk when you are about to enter the obstacle and walk them through it until they relax about it then you can start jogging them through.

The Back-Up

Always teach your horse the back-up out in the open first before you attempt putting them in between poles.

Once your horse is good at backing up straight out in an open space, place some poles running parallel with a safe fence such as an arena fence but a good distance away, it's just a visual for your horse to know that he can't try and sneak off to the side.

I like to place three fairly long rows of poles, leaving a horse length gap in the middle row so that I can use that as a back through, changing sides.

I always start them by walking **into** the back-through I won't start them at the beginning of the logs until they become accustomed of walking in and back out in a nice straight line.

Repeating this walking in, backing out several times before I have them back through the gap that has been placed in the middle row of poles. I won't start backing them through the gap until I have them backing in a straight line.

When I have repeated doing this on one side, I will move into the opposite side, getting them familiar with both sides of the back through before backing through the gap.

Backing through the middle poles

Next, I will teach them to back through the gap in the middle poles by backing them up one side, whatever side you choose to begin until their hind legs are level with the beginning of the opening.

Here is where you might have to step out of the poles (which is totally fine to do), so that you can manoeuvre your horse in through the gap.

- Turning their head toward you as you back will steer their hind end through the gap.
- Just before your horse hits the pole on the other side with his hinds, stop and stay for a bit, keeping them calm and relaxed.
- You will now have to step over the middle pole and as you do so, you will steer your horse by turning his head away from you, this will make him straighten up his hinds and get straight in his body. Stop again for a few seconds this will help him slow himself down.
- Continue the back through to the end.

Troubleshoot:

- If your horse gets crooked or gets antsy – stop! Don't keep backing up it will only make him worse if he is backed into the logs with his feet and is made to continue on. Stopping and hesitating through the whole back through will help keep them calm.
- Never try to make the entire back through into one entire back-up. Break it all down into bite-sized pieces so that it will make more sense to your horse and will be easier for

him to learn. Having him go through it in one flowing motion like you would strive for in a class will be too much for him in his early learning. It will only make him more antsy in the long run.

- If your horse is crooked in his neck – he will back crooked.

Starting the back-through from the beginning of the poles

When the time is right for moving onto backing from the beginning of the poles.

- Walk your horse around the outside of the back through obstacle, if you are coming at it from the side, walk slightly past the entrance and halt the horse when his hind feet are in the centre of the entry.
- Pivot the front-end of your horse, keeping the hind end as still as you can manage. Straighten your horse and halt. He should be as close to the middle of the gap to the entrance as you can manage and his body straight.
- When you are ready, put some pressure on your lead just under the shank of the chain and cue him to go back watching every stride is as straight as possible. Backing through until you have completed.

Troubleshoot: As mentioned above, if your horse's neck is crooked, he will back crooked so you have to be ready to straighten him up by either moving your hand that is holding the lead shank slightly to the left or right. As you move your hand to the left you will be moving his hind end right and vice-versa.

The Large Box

Again here, I teach my horse to pivot out in an open area. Don't attempt teaching a green horse that has never tried to pivot let alone pivot inside an enclosed area.

I start by standing facing my horses' left shoulder, holding the lead with my left hand about 3" from the jaw. I begin to push him away with my left hand under his jaw. I don't worry about holding onto the chain for this, once they know the drill you can bring your hand back down under the shank because you know you can't hold the chain, right?

With my right hand I will push on the horses' shoulder in unison with my left hand pushing him away from me under his jaw. Pushing on his shoulder should get him off balance in his front end, he should reach out to the right with his right leg. If this doesn't happen straight up, keep trying. If no luck in getting my horse moving I will make a fist, rather than using the flat of my hand I will push my fist (knuckles first) into his shoulder and will rhythmically push on him emphasising my knuckles – if no luck there I will use my thumb in the same manner but this time I will come off his shoulder rhythmically then bump it back onto them.

Rather than going harder and harder with my thumb sticking into his shoulder I will get quicker with my jabbing. This should get them moving.

If I get one step out of them, I stop and praise them for it before I repeat a few more times getting a step or two each time. I should then be able to get them moving enough that I can follow them. This will be the makings of my pivot.

To turn it into the pivot rather than him half walking and half moving sideways I begin to walk my body toward him level with his face, still pushing with my left hand and by this time just tapping his shoulder with my open hand I will walk into his space, he should be moving away from me with just his front end. Holding his hind end as still as he possibly can for a newbie.

At this stage I will put them in a fairly open square with the poles being quite generous to start with. Once they are at the not quite ready stage this is the time to put them in the box because now the box will help you to clean up their pivot now that there is a boundary and they have to watch where they place their feet each step.

I practice the box every day until they are pivoting quite fluently and pretty much smooth and correct. I will always go both ways when practicing this. I will do a couple of turns to the left then I will practice going to the right.

The Small Box

When you get to practicing the smaller box, you will be using the hind end along with the front.

This is because, if you tried to hold their hind end still while they moved around in the circle with their front end, you would most likely find your horse will be standing on the outside of the poles now and then.

How you stop this from happening is by dis-engaging their hind end while you move the front end (going to the left) using your corners. Dis-engage the front end and move the hind using your lead hand to shift from shoulder to hip, it's like you are moving them into the corners. You, the handler can be on the outside of the poles.

Troubleshoot: If your horse is getting too close to the poles with his hind end it is saying to me that you haven't got forward motion. You must always have your horse in a forward motion.

If they begin to stress out over this, just stop and stand for a bit. With some, you have to lead them out of the box, walk around and come back into the box, this will "unstick" their legs. They can get to feeling claustrophobic when practicing inside the small box. Take your time with working with the small box. Go back if you have to for a bit to the larger more spacious box.

Is your horse hard to catch?

This, of course, is not cool. I would imagine you would rarely strike this if you are dealing with a show horse that is turned out on a daily basis and brought back in to their stable at the end of every day. However, there are those few horses out there that are a bit difficult to catch.

Not being able to catch your horse is really frustrating. Chasing your horse down or tricking it before you start each ride is not a positive way to begin your time together.

Maybe you don't stable your horse at all, you might be collecting your horse from out of his paddock daily just to ride them and then you return him back to his paddock?

It's worth spending a little time teaching your horse to be caught. There may be a time when you absolutely must catch your horse – such as for visits from farriers and vets, or even in an emergency.

Turning out with a Halter

Generally, I don't like to turn horse's out with halters on. However, during the retraining period, you may want to keep a halter on your horse whilst out in his paddock. Horses can become entangled when trying to scratch an ear with a hind foot or can hook a halter on a gate latch and get hung up. Leather halters or halters with breakaway crowns are safer if the horse becomes entangled.

Create Positive Experiences for the Horse

If you want to be able to catch your horse, you will have to convince it that being caught doesn't always lead to discomfort or work. You'll do this by spending time with your horse that doesn't involve any of what it perceives as negative experiences.

You can do this by going in to your horse's paddock for visits with them or go in with the intention to clean up the manure or walk the fence line to check they are all ok. Do anything but go to your horse. Usually, curiosity gets the better of them and they just can't resist to come over to you to see what you are up to. If this is the case, do not try to catch him. Let your horse follow along, let him sniff you. Have it that *you* walk away from your horse and not the other way around. You always want to be the final decision-maker in any exchange with your horse.

Try and visit your horse's paddock several times a day if you can, these visits don't have to be anything in particular, just short visits to show your horse you are not interested in catching them every time you go to their paddock.

Approach the Horse Cautiously

When trying to approach your horse, don't march up to it full of purpose and intent. Instead, soften your body language and walk slowly toward your horse. Don't make direct eye contact. Don't approach head on (or tail on). Use your peripheral vision and approach at the neck or shoulder.

If the horse allows you to get near enough to catch it, spend a little time doing something enjoyable like scratching, massaging, or brushing.

When you have completed your visit – you decide the end of the visit don't let your horse decide when they should now walk off. Unhook the lead rope, make your horse stand, and then walk away from the horse.

Train the Horse in an Enclosed Area

If your horse will absolutely not allow you to get near enough to catch it, have your horse in a small, safe paddock or yard. You could use your round pen, however, this may be defeating the purpose, after all it is the "office" as far as your horse is concerned, he is going into the round yard to work!

You know your horse will run when you try to approach him, keep him moving. Use a halter and lead as an extension of your arm to cue the horse to move forward by swinging it, or without letting the halter go, fling it in the direction of your horse's hip. At the beginning your horse may act like this is fun – and run around, buck, and kick. He may even try to approach you at some point. However, don't let the horse make those decisions. If the horse tries to stop, tell it clearly and firmly to trot. When he does as you ask, praise the horse and send it on its way. Do this a few times so you know you are getting a consistent reaction to your command.

When you see that the horse is halting obediently on command, he is not stopping with his hip facing you, drop your halter and lead and approach, don't make eye contact with him. Approach by taking a few steps then turn your back on him, keep your peripheral vision on him, turn back toward him and repeat until you are about 6 feet away from him, turn away and wait to see if he will approach you. If he does, let him stand you then take a few steps away and stand again, see if he follows you. When he comes to you and stands quietly praise, scratch or pat him and walk away. Send him out at a trot again. Repeat the process until you know the horse will stand and wait for you.

DO NOT praise your horse if they stop with their haunches facing you, this is a sign of disrespect and that they are prepared to run off if you approach or, worse kick out at you if you try to approach.

Only after you know the horse will stand facing you, should you attempt to catch the horse. If it ducks away from you send it on its way and repeat the process making sure *you* are making these decisions *not* your horse.

Make sure there is a reward at the end of the lesson if he does stand for you. Put a lead rope on him and lead him to a treat in a bucket, do a little grooming, or give a massage. And then turn him loose in his paddock.

The next time you have a moment, visit the horse in the pasture or paddock. Let him learn that your appearance does not mean he has to go to work or suffer discomfort.

Note: You may need to put some work into this exercise, I have experienced with nearly every horse I have done this with they will not "come to the party" until they tire of being pushed on every time they stop.

Problems and Proofing Behaviour

If your horse only runs away when it sees you coming with a halter and lead, then always approach it with a halter and lead over your shoulder. You have to teach your horse that the appearance of the halter and lead does not mean you are going to lead it into work.

Bribing your horse with treats is only a short-term solution to your problem. You want to be able to catch your horse without carrying out a bucket or a carrot every time. And it may cause confusion among your other horses, who notice you coming with treats, and see what's in it for them.

Friendly horses in your paddocks might help you out. If they will walk up to you for pats and scratches, your hard-to-catch horse will see their behaviour and may imitate them.

Continue to visit your horse regularly and as many times as you can fit in to your day, so that it doesn't decide your appearance means unpleasant work.

Chewing on the bit

A rider was asking why her horse was chewing at the bit and whether she should go from the snaffle to a shank. I explained that I would lean toward the wolf teeth first before I would think about what sort of bit was being used.

Wolf teeth, not to be confused with Canine teeth – Canine teeth are usually found only in the mouths of male horses, including stallions and geldings. Also referred to as 'tusks', 'tushes' or 'bridle teeth', the lower canine teeth normally erupt at age four, with the upper canine teeth following at age five.

Canine teeth appear in the mouth for the purpose of fighting – as stallions compete for mares during breeding season. However, they also play a role in chewing, whereas wolf teeth do not. Interestingly, canine teeth do appear in up to 20% of mares, but they are usually very small.

What to do if your horse has wolf teeth

It makes sense to remove these potentially troublesome teeth before you attempt any serious work with your young horse. You don't want your horse to associate any discomfort or pain in his mouth with being worked. Horses can develop bad habits such chewing on the bit or head shaking, lunging their head and neck down toward the ground and twisting their heads through having long term pain, associating that pain with being ridden, creating anxiety in the horse which can go on for years before it is diagnosed as never having their wolf teeth extracted. These bad habits and anxiety can take a long time to retrain those bad habits out of the horse's mind. Wolf teeth are on the bars of the mouth and where the bit may settle. For this reason alone, they may need to be removed.

Wolf teeth can cause a young horse to fight the bit or even the pressure of a hackamore. Any pressure on the horse's cheeks is capable of rubbing on these teeth. Wolf teeth tend to be pointed, so they can cause some discomfort. Wolf teeth show up right in front of the second premolars. An individual horse may have none, one, two, or four wolf teeth. Generally, a horse with wolf teeth will have just two – both located on the upper jaw. Wolf teeth may be found in the mouths of both sexes, but the key difference is they no longer serve a purpose. Wolf teeth are the vestiges of evolution, which is why they're often called 'vestigial' or 'remnant' teeth.

The proximity of the bit to the wolf teeth often results in discomfort and pain. Wolf teeth erupt at an earlier age than canines – around six to eight months. Rarely, wolf teeth may show up as late as two to three years of age, but most yearlings obviously either have them or not. A few horses never have a problem with their wolf teeth, but many horses do. Since wolf teeth do not serve any good purpose, removing them makes good sense. They can often be blind – meaning they haven't erupted through the gum, these "blind" teeth are actually worse than the erupted wolf teeth. They can even be floating with no root attachment. For these reasons, extraction is often recommended for wolf teeth. Wolf teeth are small, peg-like teeth, which sit just in front of the first cheek teeth. Most times in my 30 odd years of training they would hide just under the surface and annoy the horse when bitted up. I would always get my dentist in before my young horses were brought in to be broken in. I would only mouth them approximately 6 months into their training, not until they had a fair idea of how to carry a rider on their backs and most of the leg and hand cues then I would think about mouthing them.

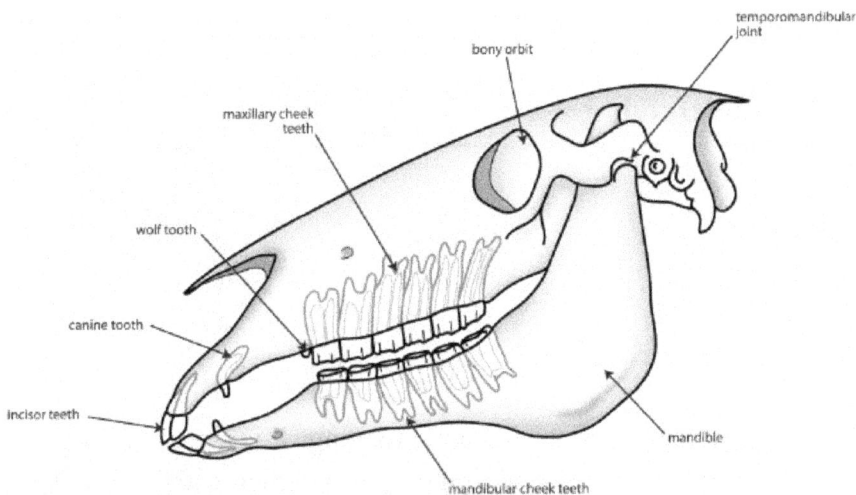

temporomandibular joint

bony orbit

maxillary cheek teeth

wolf tooth

canine tooth

incisor teeth

mandible

mandibular cheek teeth

The Equine Skull

Pesky little wolf teeth

With the wolf teeth removed it is also easier to put in a proper bit seat.

If you have an adult horse who consistently fights the bit or acts uncomfortable, it is worth having your equine dentist do a thorough exam.

Have your horses' teeth examined at least once a year.

No wolf tooth does any good and may do harm, so extract them all.

Certainly, if your horse is performing well, has no problems, and a wolf tooth finding is just an incidental, you may not want to put him through the procedure to remove the teeth. Their presence should be noted though, and if problems do show up, such as head tossing, avoiding the bit, etc, wolf teeth removal should definitely be considered.

In my experience, 9 times out of 10, having these little boogers removed was the answer to having a safe, happy, willing horse.

Ground Driving

Ground driving is similar to lunging. It is a step-up in teaching your horse how to respond to the reins and their cues before they are ridden.

Ground driving is great for developing your yearlings' gaits and balance before they have a rider on their backs.

I like to use a side-pull for this new experience, I don't like the idea of having a young horse having their mouths pulled from left to right and backwards with the bit. I introduce the bit much later in their breaking-in. If you don't have a side-pull you can, at a pinch get away with a nylon halter. I don't like using a halter, I feel they are not the correct fit for doing lots of turns and stops, they do tend to rub on their nose and cheeks.

Note: Using a side-pull is not the same as steering a horse with a snaffle in their mouths. A side-pull is exactly that, it is a SIDE – PULL, you pull an individual rein out away from the horse's face, it's not designed to pull on both reins together, all this does is run the noseband up their face and rub holes in their muzzles. If you do decide you will be using a side-pull, be sure to wrap the nose band with soft vet wrap.

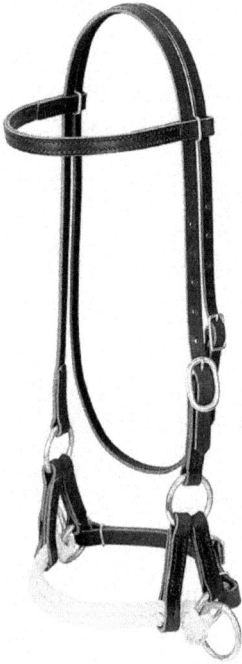

Weaver Leather Deluxe
Latigo Leather Side Pull

Western cob beta biothane
side pull with reins

Note: The bridle on the right is great for riding your young horse. I wanted to include it so that you could see the difference between the Weaver leather side-pull and the Beta Biothane side-pull – good for riding, however, not so good for driving your horse with.

Attach the long reins to the side rings on the side-pull, you can invest in a training surcingle which you can run the long reins through the side rings – NOT the rings up near the wither unless you are driving an English disciplined horse. Using those rings on the wither tends to bring the horses face in toward their chest and arching their neck. Then into your hands OR, you can save a few $

and get your young horse broken to a western saddle (ideally a light weight one). I use the saddle, I tie the oxbows together under the horse's belly, I use the oxbows to run my drive lines through – works just as good, I have driven many a future champion this way.

Tying the oxbows together underneath the horse's belly stops the individual oxbow from coming up off the side of the horse when turning them.

When teaching them to drive I like to start in the round yard where I can keep everything under control in a smaller area. I don't want them to take off suddenly and have their muzzle ripped and teared trying to pull them up when they are not used to it. Again, not necessary but be mindful of that if you are out in a large arena or out in a paddock, keep your circles small and under control.

When I think they are ready for the arena, they listen to my voice cues (especially the whoa!), they are backing up off the long reins nicely and moving up into the jog and lope calmly, I take them out into the arena, I follow directly behind them, staying at least a horse's length behind their heels.

Staying light in your hands, don't try to slow them down with pulling on both drive lines at the same time, keep turning them in one direction or the other in a serpentine fashion, this will help you slow them down and keep it all under control.

Be sure to keep him moving, if you are having trouble doing that with just clucking to them, bump them on the hip with one of the drive lines that should do it for you.

Keep your turns wide at this stage, by pulling and giving little bumps on one rein and releasing the other at the same time as if you are handing one hand over to the other, make it flow. Once your horse settles down after the turn, ask for a whoa, hold both reins with the exact same pressure, say whoa, let them walk into that pressure and hold until they take a step back. Be careful not to let your horse turn around to face you.

Get the horse going really well at the walk before you ask for the jog or lope. If at any time things go a bit crazy, bring your horse back to the walk and start over.

Backing on the drive lines

So, just like above when stopping your horse, holding the reins equally and the horse taking a step back to come off the pressure. But this time, you are wanting your horse to back more steps. To do this, use one rein at a time, pull lightly on one line and then the other to turn his head slightly back and forth then pull firmly and evenly on both lines. By pulling on one line then the other individually, will get your horse off balance a bit and it will force him to take a step to catch himself. Once you get two or three steps from him, stop a little while then walk on forward.

Circling on the driving lines

Driving in a circle allows the horse to be loped on the lines and to learn to take inside leads both directions.

When circling to the right, hold the right rein in your right hand. Have the outside line through the stirrup to keep it from slipping up over their backs. The outside line should come around just above your horse's hocks to keep the horse from facing the centre or cutting corners.

When driving in a circle, keep toward the centre but move with the horse. Begin at the walk then the jog/trot and work up to the lope/canter. If your horse is quite laid back about it all you might find it hard to get them to go into the lope. Going to the right, use your left rein (outside rein) in a swinging motion to swing it slightly around the horses back end and kiss to them, once they get into the lope stop swinging the left rein.

When asking to come back down the gaits, use your voice cues and hold both drive lines the same, putting a slight pressure on their face, as they come back down through the gaits, ease off with the pressure on the lines.

From the circle you can start to serpentine them, taking them to the left then to the right and back again. Keep the serpentines large and put your horse into a full circle here and there, mixing it up from circles to serpentines.

If you want to put them back up into the lope, get them back into the circle, ask them for the lope in the circle then moving off with them, start your serpentines in the lope. You will find you will have to run a few strides when turning them back in the other direction...just think of the good workout you will be getting!

I like to cue my horse to turn with short, gentle bumps on the side pull. If I want to cue the left turn on the serpentine. I will bump the left line. Bumping the line will keep your horse soft and responsive. If you were to hold solid on the left line your horse will try to fight with the pressure, remember, always have an "open door", pulling firmly without a release is a "closed door".

Breaking-in to ride

When the time comes to decide who will be breaking your long yearling in you can choose to do the breaking-in yourself starting with saddling and ground-driving or send them away to a professional in the field of breaking the young horses in.

The time it takes to break one in is usually around 6 weeks. I think it's a huge help for the breaker when you have had your yearling in as a halter or led performance horse teaching them the way of the world and handling them giving them confidence with humans before being sent to a stranger for breaking.

You will have completed lots of ground work with your yearling and therefore will make the breakers job flow a lot smoother than if he were to receive your horse as green as grass. His job would certainly take longer.

I know with my long yearlings and the work I put into them on the ground I was able to have my breaker take over for from 2 to 4 weeks and then I would take over from there.

I myself do not break horses in, I look at it like "one man, one job", I am a trainer, not a breaker so have always bar a few in my early days, organised my breaker to take on the job that he knew much better than I did.

I was very blessed to have a breaker that came to me and worked my young horses in my arena. I was able to oversee the work my breaker was doing and also get a really good feel of the horse's attitude, temperament and ability before it was time for me to take over.

I personally do not recommend taking this job on yourself. It can be a very dangerous task breaking a green horse, no matter how much you trust your baby with your life, it is not a good idea to take on the job of breaking in. Unless you are very experienced at it. Have a professional do the job for you, they know how and what to do, they break down the horses fears for you by putting the horse in positions that can be very un-predictable. You really need to know what you are doing when you have a blank canvas underneath you. It's not just a matter of riding them around in circles and hoping they don't buck you off.

Lots of breakers will go above and beyond for you by cracking whips from their backs, laying them down, mounting them, getting back up. They take them out into the big, scary world fearless themselves, they will make sure your horse will come back to you having had all sorts of traffic desensitising, going through and over all sorts of obstacles and terrain. Your breaker should put them through life's ringer for you and bring them back safe.

Riding the Green Broke

A green broke horse is one who has recently learned to accept a rider on his back, or to be "under saddle." But "green broke" has various shades of meaning. The only way to know what a horse knows is to spend some time with him so you can map a training path. At a minimum, you know he's inexperienced.

Now that you have your horse back from the breakers it is important to continue where the breaker left off. Don't be tempted to put your horse out for a spell thinking he deserves some time off after all the work he must have been through. Now is the time for you to take over straight away, this will also be good for you and your confidence. Hopefully, you have had a ride on your horse when you went to pick him up or at the very least have been watching progress videos to give you a bit of insight on what you will be getting to work with.

Serpentines

Serpentine's are a series of 'S' turns. Guiding your horse with one rein, the direct rein, steering the horse off a straight line of movement. Alternating from one rein to the other, handing the rein over in a smooth, flowing motion. Serpentines are excellent exercises for young horses and also riders because the frequent changes of direction require concentration from both horse and rider and accuracy in the aids.

This lesson is one of the foundations for any kind of performance horse.

Serpentine's are something I do from the very first ride. It is a daily routine throughout the horse's life. It is not very often you will find me riding in a straight line, I know sometimes straight lines are definitely necessary but as a rule my foundation training is riding serpentine's, figure 8's, multi circle serpentines as I call them.

Some riders use the serpentine as a precise drill, ensuring the half circles are done exactly the same size and shape. I don't use them like that, I use the serpentine as a training aid to help with keeping the shoulders up, slowing my horse's rhythm down and create suppleness in my horses. Where I choose to change direction is of no consequence, I will change direction from the 'feel' I get from my horse as well. If I need to change direction because the horse is dropping a shoulder or feels unbalanced or if the horse feels racy and needs to slow its mind or, simply just to change direction to keep the horse from speeding up in his legs.

The first thing I do when taking over from the breaker is the serpentine at all gaits. There are a couple of reasons why I do this:

1. Doing serpentine's, as opposed to riding your horse in either a straight line or a continuous circle is going to help keep the horses mind on you, the rider.
2. For balance. Frequent changes of direction teach a horse not to drift, lean or drop their shoulder through the turn. These exercises improve the balance of both horse and rider.
3. Keeps the horse from dropping the shoulder. If you were riding a circle continuously, the horse will begin to tire and start dropping their shoulder into the direction they are travelling. Serpentine's stop this from happening as there is always a change in direction the horse needs to lift the shoulder to take the weight of the turn.
4. Serpentine's take the "predictable" out of the equation, your horse won't know exactly where they will be going next,

they have to rely on you to show them the direction they are to go in.

5. We can redirect a horse's nervous energy telling the horse where to put his feet, we then take control of the situation.
6. For speed control. The horse has to slow down in order to change direction.
7. For gaining low head carriage. A horse will normally lower their head to balance through the turn.
8. Serpentine's will often show up any favouring of one side to the other in your horse.

Starting with a basic serpentine

Although you will ride with one rein at a time with this exercise, you should always have light contact on the opposite rein. If your non-working rein is draped 1. A no, no with a green broke horse to have draped reins, 2. If your non-working rein is draped and you want to change rein, you will be snatching at your horse's mouth leaving one rein and putting the pressure on the opposite rein. This will probably frighten your horse if you snatch at him rather than blend from one rein to the other.

My personal preference for type of head gear when starting a green horse is the Side-Pull, it's not necessary for you to use one if you aren't familiar with one and how they are used you could quite easily turn your serpentine riding into a disaster. If you are happier with a snaffle that's fine. More than likely your breaker would have mouthed your horse up with a snaffle and he should be well used to it. My thinking on using a side-pull on a green horse is they don't also have the stress of worrying about a bit in their mouths being pulled this way and that along with getting used to carrying a rider, getting their balance and learning the body cues that are coming from the rider.

I like to wait until they get stronger in their balance, they are obeying my seat, leg, feet and voice cues before I introduce a snaffle.

Once I do introduce the snaffle bit to the young horse, he is pretty much working off my lower body cues and voice. It helps create a soft mouthed horse.

Ride in a large area where you can change direction often. Start by walking your horse in a fairly large circle to the left. When you are about to change directions, hold that left rein and with your right hand begin to take up more tension on the right rein, while your right hand is doing this let your left rein slacken slightly, remember, you don't want to drape that rein. This should be done all in one movement so that there is no quick, sudden jerking on your horse's mouth from one rein to the other. Your cue has commenced for the right turn of your serpentine.

When changing rein, say you are going to change from the left rein to the right, you should run your right hand down the right rein, tightening your grip of your fingers around the rein and guide the rein out away from your horse's neck. Your right elbow should be no further back than your side but away from your body, bending at the elbow, guide the horses face around to the right using your hand as a 'pointer', (I will even point my index finger out to the right) let your horse see your hand out there guiding him like an indicator to go right. When he changes direction relax your grip slightly but keep on guiding him with your right rein until it's time to go left.

You should never have two slack reins in this exercise, if you're going left, your left rein and arm are the indicator and vice-versa for the right.

Continue making a series of left and right half-circles making up your S shapes. Keep the half circles big, you don't want to be doing short, quick half circles, keep them a decent size, using up the entire arena.

As the horse follows his nose, allow him to walk freely, bumping him with the sides of your legs gently and rhythmically giving him the cue to keep moving forward.

Keeping an eye on that inside shoulder to make sure he is not dropping in to the inside, if he is it means he is dropping his shoulder in the direction of travel. It is imperative that you **change reins immediately** to stop him from dropping his shoulder and it becoming a habit.

Do this same exercise at the trot always ride with rhythm. If you ride with a nice even rhythm your horse will naturally come back to that rhythm and you will be "one unit".

<u>Troubleshoot:</u>

- If your horse's nose turns but he continues walking straight ahead, use both legs bumping his sides and cluck to him to speed up slightly. When his shoulders begin to follow his nose direction for one or two steps, release the rein just enough to let him know you are still guiding him in that direction and soften your leg bumps.

Note: I like to continue bumping them lightly with my legs, I find it relaxes them and lets them know you are still there. I don't like to suddenly appear with my legs on a young horse, it can frighten them if it is sudden and unexpected. My rhythm is not fast at all and is minimal pressure, just enough to keep them rocking along and knowing I am there.

Advancing in the serpentine

Once you are confident that you and your horse have got these walk, jog serpentine's down pat, it's time to introduce the canter.

Moving up a gait is always going to have a bit more degree of difficulty with it. It's just the way it is, moving from the walk up to the jog is going to be a little more challenging, you will need to concentrate more on the speed at which you take a hold of your horses face at the jog as opposed to the walk. You will have to be on the ball to not allow yourself to follow the horse's rhythm, especially a young green horse that is more than likely going to be a little quicker in his movement than what we are looking for. You will need to get your rhythm and the horse is to come back to you not the other way around.

Cantering the serpentine is going to give you an open door to getting the lope on your horse in a shorter period of time and a more natural lope into the bargain!

Like I said above, moving up the gaits there is a degree of difficulty at the canter, you will be pushing your horse on with your legs in a bumping rhythm, you will be opening up the top half of your body which may feel a little vulnerable while you are cantering around on a young horse or, maybe an older horse that has no experience in serpentines. It may be a bit un-co for a while and feel a little bumpy at first however, you are in this for a reason and that reason is to train your horse and have him ready for the show pen down the track.

The canter

I like to be in a jog or trot if the horse is not quite jogging just yet when I am starting a young horse at this. I know I have just finished explaining how going *up* through the gaits there is a little more degree of difficulty, however, that relates to the rider *not* so much the horse in this particular exercise.

Riding your horse at the jog or trot in your serpentine, begin your half circle but until you get your horse into a canter stay in the circle, we will use the left lead in this example. Make your circle slightly smaller than that of the walk and jog serpentine, this will keep things under control, you will be keeping your horse's body in an arc to the left, this is a much safer way to get your horse into a canter than trying to get them to canter from a straight line.

You should already be bumping (I like to call it "sacking out") your lower part of your leg at the horse's side in that rhythmic, soothing motion. When you want to move up a gait all that is required is to start bumping your leg and your heel a little firmer with the bumps. Kiss to your horse to cue for the canter.

When you have got your horse up into the canter, keep sacking those legs of yours to not only keep him up in the canter but to continue that repetition and confidence that you have been doing all along...don't change it now, keep up the continuity. Also, once in the canter you want to make your circle bigger now than when you were holding him in an arc. Let him canter at his own speed *DO NOT* try slowing him down to a show lope, this will come later, naturally.

Do two or three large circles to the left, when you are feeling comfortable and ready for your first change in direction repeat exactly what you did with your cues in the walk and trot, crossing over evenly from the left rein to the right. Continue cantering on for two or three large circles then go back to the left rein, then back to the right. Be sure to read the "Troubleshoot" below.

Note: At this stage you may not be riding with spurs, that is fine for now if that makes you feel safer. However, if you are using spurs, when sacking out your legs, let the spurs occasionally touch your horse's side, it's not necessary to use them every stride. Just enough to encourage them to get up into the canter.

Troubleshoot:

- Fast trotting: If your horse wants to trot faster before he canters off, this is ok for a little while but you want to make sure you nip it in the bud before it becomes second nature to trot fast before going up a gait. In the beginning stages, it is all about balance and co-ordination for a young horse it can be a big step for them initially. – Don't let it keep up for too long though.

If you are going to canter off on the left lead for example and your horse takes the right lead, you should do one of two things –

1. Alter your direction of going so that your horse is on the right lead doing a right circle.
2. Drop back to the trot and ask again for the left lead canter.

- Again, this is in the early stages of training I prefer to drop the horse back to a trot and asking for the correct lead, however, depending on the horse's attitude and ability, it is sometimes better to ride your horse into a right lead canter. You have to keep in mind that your young horse is in kindergarten, you can't expect everything to be perfect. You are, I hope, a teacher *without* an iron rod to chastise with at every wrong move.

- When you change direction from the left lead circle to the right, if your horse stays on the left lead this is totally fine, as a matter of fact, it is great! Your horse staying on that left lead when you change directions is now working on his 'counter canter'. He doesn't yet know this but this will be one of his main exercises that he needs to use in his training regimen.

- If he does stay on his left lead don't do several circles with him, he will deteriorate super-fast if you keep him going, just swing around back to the left after you have done a half circle or maybe get a full circle out of your horse in the counter-canter.

- If, however, he does change leads either by a flying lead change (well aren't you a lucky bugger!), or he drops down into a trot, this is also not an issue. When I am doing the serpentine in the canter on a young horse, I go with the flow so to speak. I ignore the break of gait and the lead that the horse chooses at the change of rein, if he changes his lead or stays on the same lead at this stage it is nothing to worry about at this early stage of his training.

Flexing at the poll

Before you begin this lesson

Before you begin, you can either lunge your horse to loosen him up and relax him or hop on, do some trotting serpentines around your arena for ten or fifteen minutes this will help get them ready for the day's lesson. I don't like riding a horse in mindless circles when I am warming them up, I like to shift from rein to rein when warming up. Serpentines are a great tool to supple your horse. A horse is more supple doing serpentines than bopping around in a mindless, boring circle. Don't think for a minute though that circles don't come in handy as a training tool depending on what's going on in the lesson.

There's a lot to be said about ground work – lunging, not only does it warm your horse up physically, it also helps prepare their minds for your ride. Lunging is also a great way to gauge their attitude on the day.

Don't leave out some groundwork exercises to get your horse relaxed first, get your horse ready mentally as well as warming him up. The more ground work you do during the period you're working on flexion, the more quickly he'll progress. There's nothing worse than working on an exercise and your horse is too fresh in the mind to want to join you.

While working on this lesson get your horse in a properly fitted snaffle bit. Making sure there are no teeth or bit problems before you start, I'm picking that you will have little success if your horse's teeth are giving him problems so it's a good idea to make sure you have had the dentist in to see if there are any problems in there. You don't want those Wolf teeth left in there that's for sure.

If you're dealing with a horse that has no clue on how to flex at the poll and give to your cues, remember to be patient. Take whatever time is needed to teach your horse to flex at a standstill, then move up the gaits, always using enough leg pressure at the same time to let him know you don't mean slow down – you mean "give."

A horse that raises his head instead of giving to your hands is trying to escape from your vertical flexion cue. This could be due to lots of different reasons, including teeth problems, bad training in the past or an ill-fitting or pinching bit. Let's say, he's had his teeth seen to and the bit isn't a problem, it's easy for a horse to hang on to bad habits from the past. Some of these bad habits they learn through various reasons, it can be a long-term process to correct. This is why it requires time and patience from you.

You will always give back to him by softening on the pull of the reins.

To be effective, this method must become a consistent routine until you recondition your horse's response. In the end, you will teach your horse that if he gives to your hands by flexing at the poll when you pick up on the reins and apply some pressure, you will always give back to him by softening on the pull of the reins as his reward.

Timing

The timing of your release is very important. As soon as your horse gives to your pressure on the reins even if it's a small gesture initially, you have to have the "feel" to know to release your pressure.

Repetition is imperative with any training you give your horse so you will repeat the process. Strive for a bit more response over time. You will know by your horse's response – *or not* – as to when to *give*.

Remember to work on this at a standstill before you move on to asking for flexion at the walk, jog and lope especially if your horse has problems in this area.

Here's how

Horse's usually favour one side over the other just like we are left or right handed. I like to pick their good side to work on first to start with so that I am not causing any confusion or making life harder for both of us trying to teach them on their bad side first. After a while it doesn't usually matter which side you start and finish on. You want to make life easier for both of you though in the beginning then you can mix it up after that to keep him guessing and never assuming it's right first then left otherwise, he will go through the motions before you even get a chance to put any pressure on.

I will use the left rein as the good side in this example.

Run your left hand down the rein slightly and hold some pressure there until you feel your horse giving to that pressure, you should also notice that he is flexing at the poll and bringing his chin closer to the point of the left shoulder.

You might find that your horse may pull on your hand pressure, this is where I would tell you to "sit your ground", don't release the rein in your response and don't pull on his mouth, just stay where you are with your hand pressure and wait for him to give.

If you feel that you can't keep your hand steady on his mouth try placing your hand on your hip for a bit of a brace and to stop you from moving back and forth with your horses' actions. Once you feel your horse "giving" even a small but clear response, you will see a slight flex at his poll and a lowering of his head, release your pressure on the reins by opening your fingers and giving your horse a release on the rein. This is his reward for giving his face. Your horse will soon learn to give to you getting his reward *from you* at the *precise* time that he gives.

Your work is not done

If you found you got a great result the first time, don't assume you are going to breeze through this lesson. Depending on where you're at, it's not always smooth sailing every time.

Your horse may resist the next attempt and may raise his head to try and escape the "hold" on the rein. He may even get his head and neck up even higher than the first time thinking he's worked it all out and get away from the pressure. Same again, "sit your ground", be patient here and wait for the flex in his poll.

You will find the more you practice this lesson, the longer he will stay slightly flexed even once you have released the pressure on the reins. It may only be a little here and there. Ultimately, you will be striving for your horse to stay slightly flexed at the poll and his chin heading toward the "left" (in this instance) point of the shoulder.

Once you feel that your horse is responding well on his good side move on over to the right and repeat everything you did on the left side. Keeping in mind that he may not be as keen if this new side is his weaker side so be patient and wait for him to give to your pressure **sit your ground.**

What I wouldn't do and why

- Flow from the left rein to the right in one movement
- lean into my working hand with my body weight
- use sharp, snatching movements
- reprimand the horse **severely** for pulling away from my hand
- lose my cool if what I'm doing is not going to plan
- try to bring the horses head right back to the point of shoulder from the get-go

Flowing from the left rein to the right in one movement

This is just aggravating to the horse swinging from side to side. It's not giving him time to gather his thoughts and learn anything by mindlessly going from side to side. I like the horse to *"take in"* what he is learning. If you choose to sway from side to side down the track that's not so bad but I like to teach a horse **one side at a time**

The soft feel you'll begin to obtain with this exercise can, given additional training, eventually turn into true collection. The softness and responsiveness throughout your horse's body that makes him a true pleasure to ride.

Lean into my working hand with my body weight

If you lean down with your body weight to follow your working hand that is running down the rein all of that weight is now pushing down on the horse's front end making it much harder for him to be soft and supple in the front end.

Be aware of your body position – don't lean forward even though your arm is moving down the rein, sit up try not to lean left or right with your body also as this will make it harder for your horse, he now has to catch your body weight as well as flex.

Use sharp, snatching movements

This is going to either light a fire under your horses' belly or make him very nervous and frightened. He won't be concentrating on you or the lesson if he is in that predicament. Keep your movements soft and rhythmic.

Reprimand the horse severely for pulling away from your hand

Again, this is only going to cause your horse to be frightened or nervous, horses don't tend to retain anything when they are in fight or flight mode. Imagine trying to learn a times table and there's someone there threatening to whoop you if you get one of them wrong! I reckon I'd be hard pressed to retain those times tables!

Lose your cool if what your doing is not going to plan

Remember my quote above –

"sit your ground"

This basically means just wait it out, don't lose your cool. If your horse is refusing to give, be patient and wait. If you attempt to do this time and time again and your horse won't be in it. **Don't lose your cool.**

Where there's a will there's a way, I never like to try and put a square peg into a round hole. Just because 9 out of 10 horses can work this out fairly quickly doesn't mean that 10th horse will.

I really can't stress enough…*Patience is the virtue here.*

Don't try to bring the horses head right back to the point of shoulder from the get-go

Always baby steps at the beginning especially if your horse has no education or very little in this area.

Collection

I drive my horses into the bit to encourage collection. The more collected your horse is, the slower he can go. Lifting and driving your horse teaches them to stay slow and helps them develop self-carriage. This is a great exercise to get your horse to round their back and to reach with their legs.

I do this by lifting both reins up at the wither until I get contact with their mouths then I take a touch more rein until my horse gives to my pressure in the bit. If he resists this or tries pulling the reins from my hands, I will bump lightly to bump him off the bridle while I'm encouraging him forward with my leg. My favourite exercise is to medium trot my horse under light contact encouraging him to drive up deep underneath himself and lift up and round his back. This develops long, slow, soft steps while reaching deep behind. When I really feel my horse roll up underneath me, I may like to release my rein pressure and feel him slow down into a slow, rhythmic jog. I may also two-track at the trot from one corner diagonally across the arena to the other corner, while still driving and collecting my horse. If after these exercises your horse thinks go, simply stop and roll your horse back. Continue the lift and drive exercises.

Pretty Backing

I recently had someone comment on how horses in the show pen are not backing up when asked by the rider while presenting to the judge. They all showed resistance, opened mouths and did not back straight. It was mentioned that even the horses in Bosals threw their heads up. There was no softening of the poll.

Every horse should back willingly on cue. It demonstrates a certain amount of obedience and submission to the rider's aids.

A lot of the time, riders don't put enough training time into backing their horses up focussing on its correctness, riders tend to back their horses up at the end of the lesson a few strides and call it a day.

Backing with purpose is a very important manoeuvre which can sometimes be the difference between winning the class or being second.

Judges will use the backup to help them decide their final placings in the class, their notepad may for example have two competitors running neck and neck for first place, it will then be decided by the backup on who will take home 1st place. Again, the judge is looking for a responsive horse that is going to show willingness to the riders' subtle cues.

The foundation for a good back up:

- is ensuring your horse is responsive to your cues such as leg pressure,
- be trained to "give" or yield to pressure from the bit. in two ways:
- 1. By flexing at the poll when you pick up contact with both reins,
- 2. By bending laterally (side to side) when you pick up contact using one rein at a time. Without this amount of suppleness, he'll likely lock his jaw and lean on the bit, resulting in a hopeless tug of war.

Practicing the backup should be a daily routine and done in repetition throughout the course of your training time, focussing on correct body alignment each time.

One reason that can come in to play when it's your turn to present your backup to the judge only to find all of your hard work and dedication has just been blown out the window -waiting in the line-up for your turn, if it's been a big day or a large class and there are a few in the line-up, your horse may have started to take his five minutes unofficial break and start to relax, when your turn has come and you feel under pressure to suddenly show your backing skills, the nerves may have taken over, your reactions speed up and it's all systems go! This then causes a bad reaction in your horse and hence the resistance that you will get from your horse, don't forget he is taking what he feels is his well-deserved break to be suddenly pulled into gear. Be prepared and plan ahead, don't use this time in the line-up to talk to your fellow competitors taking your focus off the job at hand. "it aint over till it's over".

The closer you get to "show day" the more *finesse* should be put into it.

The take home…

- Teach your horse to be supple and responsive to your cues;
- practice backing your horse daily with purpose, including it into all of your stops, don't just unconsciously back a few strides and move on to something else;
- "finesse" your backup by getting your cues to look as subtle as possible;
- Be prepared, think ahead, stay focussed on the task at hand, don't rush when it is finally your time to shine!

A Little Off Topic Note: …

It's a similar predicament to the jog/trot down through the centre of the pen focussing on your straight lines and loose rein.

You would be amazed on how difficult this can be if you don't incorporate it into your daily training especially when you know that you may be asked to jog or trot down through the middle of the pen before the class starts. It's another *finesse* you need to check on daily to be confident that you will be able to perform it on the day. I doubt you would ever be asked to perform this at your local show however, no harm in broadening your experience!

Draw Reins

I like to get the draw reins on and use them to help the horse gain balance and self-carriage. That's one use for draw reins. I also put them on if I'm going to be working on transitions like the lope because there can be quite a bit of hand to mouth contact in setting the horses body parts up to take a lope transition, along with correcting and re-shaping the horse's body. When used properly, they are a good training aid. Used improperly, they can cause problems.

It's not wise to over-use draw reins or to use them just to get a horse's head down. People sometimes use draw reins for that very reason, they forget about the rest of the horse's body and balance. All this does is put the horse on the forehand. You really need to think about the horse's *self*-carriage. When a horse has "self-carriage," the horse literally carries his weight (including the rider's weight) balanced over his haunches. Because he's balanced on the hindquarters, he has a light, lifted front end and a soft poll. He carries his weight without leaning on the rider's hands, he moves upright and light.

If you only use them to get the horse's head down, you'll lose the horse's natural movement. You see horses in draw reins where their chins are to their chests, and they are just shuffling around, flopping on their front ends without any natural carriage or lift to their bodies, once a horse learns to move in this way, it's hard to correct and keep them off the forehand because most horses *prefer* to place their weight over their shoulders.

When you begin training with the draw reins you will require: -

- A smooth snaffle, bridle
- Draw Reins
- Work Boots (at least on the forelegs)
- Your Western Saddle and pad
- Girth

1. Using a **smooth snaffle** for the lessons in draw reins is what is required here.
2. **Draw Reins**...of course.
3. **Work boots** are always very important when riding your horse for a myriad of reasons, especially young horses when they are still making bone and their joints are still open. In this lesson especially because you will be moving the forehand around a fair bit. You don't want your horse to be knocking his legs around and standing on himself, marking and hurting his legs.
4. Now you don't necessarily have to be riding in a western **saddle** if you don't have one, **however**...
5. The **girth** must be the type with a ring that sits directly underneath the horse. This will be where you will clip the draw reins for the first ride or two. I keep my eye on the shape of my horse's head and neck at this point. If my horse is showing me, he is very soft and responsive in the draw reins by trying to hide behind the bit or over bending in his neck and lowering his head, I will bring the reins up to the ring on the side of the girth or to the rigging ("D") on the saddle. This change is very dependent on the horse and their responsiveness to the draw reins.

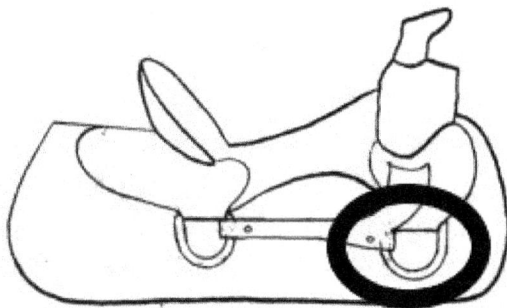

Saddle Rigging

Be sure your horse knows how to yield to your leg cues. You will be going into some of the calisthenic exercises

You will find when you are giving your horse a workout where you are moving different body parts, how you can use the exercises as individual helpers to fix a certain body part. Draw reins will help keep your hands soft on your horse's mouth.

When your horse has these manoeuvres down pat, you can certainly use them individually when you feel the need. Your horse may be sticking a bit with his shoulders, you will be able to throw him into a "move the shoulder" exercise on the rail, do two or three 360 circles and lope off again. The draw reins will make it easier for you and your horse in the early stages of his training.

As with anything, when you use draw reins, there should be a give-and-take in the rider's hands. You pick up, feel him come to the collected frame and then release immediately. But if you have the draw reins really short and you're driving a horse's head down with a constant hold, he might keep self-carriage for a while, but eventually, he's just going to lay on his front end.

Teaching a horse collection and position, you have to release the reins so the horse can learn to carry himself, this is known as "self-carriage". The horse should not learn to rely on a firm hold that is pulling his front end into the ground. A horse *will* lean on the bit over time.

In my training program I like to start my young horse's in a side-pull. I stay with the side-pull for some time while they are getting used to carrying my weight and learning my leg cues. I like to let the young horse develop self-carriage and balance without any question of them leaning on the bit. Breaking a young horse in going into the snaffle from the get go is fine if that is what you prefer to do, it's been done that way for hundreds of years, I prefer to use the side-pull before introducing the snaffle because it is just one less thing the young horse has to get used to when he is being broken-in. The snaffle bit whether it is used first up or after the side-pull is going to be foreign to your horse, but they will have come a long way without the snaffle with me before they need to feel a foreign piece of cold steel in their mouths. There is an added bonus in training with the side-pull too and that is a shorter period of time getting them accustomed to the snaffle being in their mouths. You will have done all the ground work already with them, teaching them to go left and right, to back up to jog and lope all in the side-pull while ground driving not to mention 30 to 60 days of being ridden in the side-pull, having developed (hopefully by this time) good balance, speed control and trust. It is then just a matter of getting your horse used to carrying a snaffle. This is a simple procedure of placing a snaffle hung loosely in their mouths for a few days, allowing them to 'hold' the snaffle by gathering up the slack and holding it in a comfortable position. I do this while they are tied up waiting to be worked. I tie them up from the halter, put a headstall/bridle on them that has a soft, rubber snaffle attached. Leaving the snaffle hang down a fraction longer than it should be in the horse's mouth to encourage them to pick it up and hold it. This is done for five days to a week, holding the snaffle while they are waiting for me on the tie-up.

When my young horse is ready for the snaffle it is just a matter of taking him back a few steps, back to ground driving for a little bit to let him get used to the different feel of a snaffle bit and how it works differently on the sides of his mouth. It naturally doesn't take as long as his first experience with ground driving in the side-pull, however, you have to go back to ground driving in the snaffle as it is a total new experience for them. If you go down the same road as me with your horse and decide to start your horse in a side-pull, you will find that your horse will *temporarily* flounder for a little bit, he will be a bit slower at turning to the left or right on your cue to do so, he will be frozen to the ground when asked to back when he was backing like a rock star for you in the side-pull. Just because he has been ground driven for quite some time in the side-pull does not mean he will be the same when introducing the snaffle.

When it's time to start riding the horse after you have given him time on the drive lines introducing the snaffle, I will go straight into using the draw reins, I can be lighter on their face as opposed to direct hand to mouth contact. Remembering that the snaffle is new to them, they will need time in learning the new 'feel' of the snaffle. I will stay with handing over one rein to the other as I do my serpentines. I won't be holding both sides of his face at the same time and pulling back on both reins at once.

I stay with the draw reins longer on a young or green horse than I would if I was using them on a seasoned horse to fix a transition for example. I think they are a very good tool for the purpose of guiding the young or green horse through their training while they develop the knowledge of how to carry themselves – and the rider. I don't want the seasoned horse to learn to use them as a training crutch. At some point, you do have to remove them, you should never rely on them as a crutch.

Where do they go

Initially, I will clip the draw reins to the ring on the underside of the girth, being sure to have the reins on the *outside* of their front legs, if they are clipped on going *through* their front legs tends to put the horse on his front end. *See the picture below for the correct placement.*

I spoke about the usefulness of draw reins and the problems that can occur when you overuse them. I will use draw reins on a seasoned horse when I am teaching them something like the lope transition or, maybe they need to be reminded how to hold their frame, I feel I can get this with a lot softer pressure on their mouths when the draw reins are used.

When you're teaching a manoeuvre to your horse, especially a young one, the least amount of undue steering, pulling and jerking on their mouths the better, it is going to be hard enough for the horse to learn and absorb the lesson on soft hands (which the draw reins give you) as opposed to "direct" hand to mouth contact.

This is a no brainer for me if I'm training a young one, however, I will use draw reins on older horses too for this lesson. It doesn't matter if a horse is a 6-year-old or over, it is not a *given* that he should be ridden with a shank bit, you can put him back in the draw reins, it will only help to sharpen him up.

There are many different types of draw reins, I prefer the fine, rolled leather draw reins or even the cord draw reins are good. I find the shorter draw reins are much easier to use, the longer type can be a bit of a hassle when trying to take out the slack in a hurry. The shorter reins glide easier from one hand to the other without creating long loops that can tend to get caught on the horn of the saddle.

Weaver rolled leather draw reins

When using draw reins, you can leave your normal split reins on along with the draw reins. Some rider's like to do this to get what they are asking of the horse with the draw reins then they will revert back to their split reins until they need to "correct" again. I personally don't like doing this simply because it is a mad mess! Far too much going on with reins everywhere. I would rather take the full lesson using the draw reins, choosing to use the split reins on their own in a different lesson. Some rider's think that using both sets of reins together will be a smoother transition into using direct hand to mouth contact once the horse is ready to upgrade to split reins.

Incorrect

You will notice above; the draw reins have been placed **between** the horse's front legs. This is ok if you are training dressage, it is not correct for the western trained horse, it will put them on the forehand and give them too much arch in their necks.

Your daily workout routine

For the ultimate supple, responsive horse, I like to use a form of calisthenics exercises. Calisthenics is basically a routine of blending the exercises of certain body parts in to one flowing movement.

I changed my program many years ago after I had a few clinics with my mentor – Cleve Wells. I watched this man do calisthenics on his horses and was blown away on how soft and supple it made them. I watched Cleve totally alter a horse that I had in training from fair to middling to absolute world beater! He changed his way of going (for the better) within a matter of 15 or 20 minutes, the horse looked like he was ready to win the Senior horse pleasure at the World! It blew me away. I couldn't wait to try it on my other horses and sure enough, within one or two rides, my horses felt so soft, so responsive and moved with so much cadence and lift. I love Cleve's method of calisthenics, once your horse can flow in and out of the exercises you are able to use them whenever and wherever you are as a 'fix' for dropped shoulders, speed control, elevation, correcting the top-line, dragging their back end along, you name it, if your horse starts to lose his cadence, you can stop what you're doing wherever you are, be it on the rail or in the centre, out in an open paddock or in the warm up pen you put them into a calisthenics workout for a few minutes, balance them and get back to what you were doing. It is the best way by far to teach your horse to stay upright and balanced. You don't necessarily have to combine every body part every time you want to correct something once they have been trained with this method, but you do need to teach them the procedure of blending all of the body parts together.

Because I am putting the horse through a series of exercises that flows from one to the other, the horse needs to be fit and have good balance and staying power, he needs to move effortlessly without hesitation in his movement.

While performing these manoeuvres, the draw reins are good to use to ensure that your hand to mouth contact is soft and smooth. This way, you can concentrate on your horse's body knowing that he has less pressure on his mouth. Once they are excellent in their movements flowing together seamlessly you can ride them with direct hand to mouth contact.

You will see in this picture below how supple the horse is in the draw reins. If you use the draw reins correctly, your horse freely accepts them, he will become more pliable.

Soft and pliable

Breaking it all down

Teaching your horse these flowing exercises for control, and the ability to *blend* these four exercises into one is essential for the rider to break down individually so that your horse can fully understand what you're asking of him.

It is also essential that your horse knows how to yield off your legs.

Imagine learning the steps of a dance in this case, the instructor would naturally teach you one move perhaps for that day's lesson, then when they see that you have it down pat then they know it's time to move on to the next stage of the dance routine. Your instructor would never expect you to be able to go through the whole dance routine without practising all of the necessary moves individually.

The four exercises that I teach here are: -
- Moving the **shoulder** in a Counter Arc
- Moving the **hip** in the same arc
- **Side pass**
- **Backup**

These exercises will be done individually at first, they will eventually be blended into one smooth, rhythmic manoeuvre.

Here's what you need to know

- The Counter Arc- Move the shoulder

The counter arc is a movement where your horse is travelling to the left, however, his head and neck will be held to the right, he will be facing away from the direction of travel.

- What is going on with the forehand when moving the shoulder.

What I mean by this is say if you are moving to the left, the right front leg is going to be crossing over the left front, initially, in your training this move, your horse may only move his right leg over toward his left. This is ok at the start, keep working on this until you have your horse crossing his right front leg over his left front.

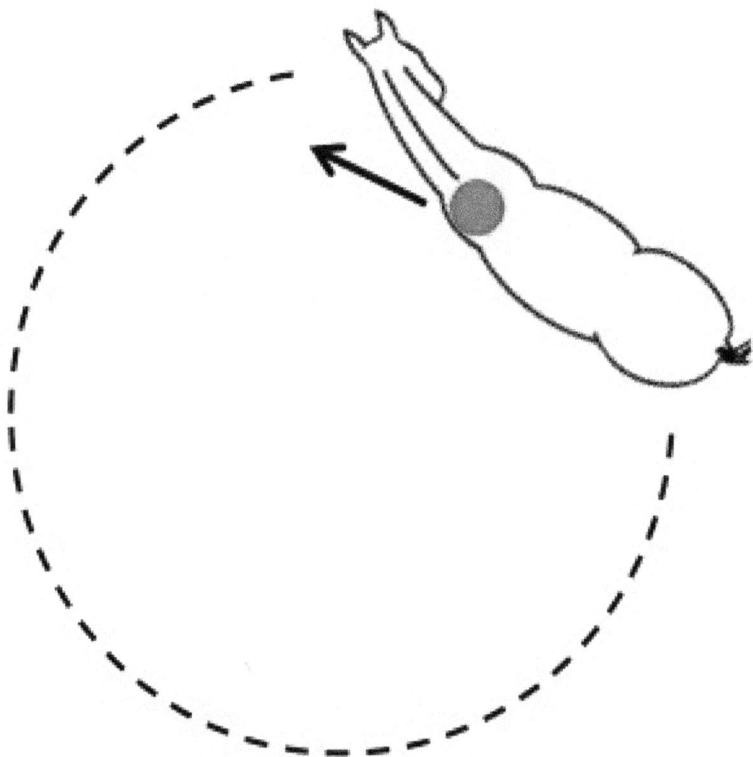

Ideally, when your horse has perfected these exercises, you want to be able to cross that right front over the left front from the horse's <u>shoulder</u>, not just from the elbow. Remember at first, when they are learning this you will ask for the move from the elbow, from that, you can take it up a notch getting your horse to cross over that front left from the shoulder. This is a matter of pushing that right leg over the left from high up in *your* right leg. Pushing all the way down from your butt cheek to your heel or spur exaggerating that push.

As you push firmly with your right leg it will shift your body toward the left of your horse. When your horse's right leg is midway across, it should feel like your horse needs to reach further with that right leg to catch your weight.

- Side-pass

With the horse in a slight bend (not straight this time).

When doing the side-pass, I keep my horse in the same shape, (head and neck to the right in this example). If I am coming off the left direction shoulder exercise, all I need do is shift my right leg slightly back from where I have been moving his shoulder over and begin the left direction side-pass.

- Moving the hip

Again, I will move the hip while still in the same counter arc. If I have the horse's head and neck to the right moving the shoulder over to the left, the only difference in my or the horse's shape is that I will take my right leg off, using my left leg now behind the girth pushing the hip over to the right, – same direction as the horse's head and neck are placed.

If the shoulder is moving to the left, I will move the hip to the right. If the shoulder is being moved to the right, I will move the hip to the left. The only time I will do both shoulder and hip in the same direction is if they are broken up by a backup or a side pass in between.

- Backing your horse

Backing your horse is the only time I have the horse straight in these particular manoeuvres. I hold both reins evenly and simply pull them back, while squeezing my legs down through to my heel or I will go to my spur if I don't get a response from the heel. I want my horse to back clean and be responsive, no feet dragging or hesitating midway through the manoeuvre.

These individual exercises can now be blended into one. Know when to quit the exercises and jog out for a break. Knowing when to "give" back to your horse and when to stay in the manoeuvres.

Why do you need to do these workout exercises daily?

It's is the best way to get your horse responsive, respectful, fit and "show ready". These exercises are a great way to keep your horse honest.

The four body parts should be constantly swapped around, it stops the horse from anticipating the next move. You need to keep your horse guessing so that they don't learn to do these exercises on their own. This will have them just go through the motions.

I see lots of riders when warming up their horses before a class, lesson or clinic, whatever they are getting ready for, will always repeat their warm-up regimen to the letter every time. After a period of time your horse will take over the controls and go 'auto-pilot' on you. You don't want a horse to find out about this 'auto-pilot', trust me it's very hard for them to un-learn it. Like riding a bike, they never forget and will always, somewhere along the line revert back to it because it's an easier road for them. After all, they created these auto-pilot short-cuts.

These short-cuts include leaning forward, dropping the shoulder by leaning into the centre of the circle, not driving from behind, hollowing out in the back, or he takes his own good time at it. He thinks as long as he's going through the motions, he will be fine. The easiest way to not let this happen is to combine the above four exercises into one fluent movement and alternating the body parts. Always changing it up, never doing the exercise in the same way each time. Keep your horse in the dark, keep him guessing and that will create a more responsive, honest horse – he has to follow your lead or he will mess up the dance steps.

The more seasoned horse

When you have been doing these exercises in a flowing movement on your horse and he is handling it really well, it's time to speed it up and really blend all four of those body parts together as one. Don't stop for a break, have a plan in your head on what body part you are going to bring after the one you are working on now. If you think your horse may be getting a bit heated up about it and starts showing he is trying to find a hole to escape out of, it's time to jog or lope off, let him lope on a lose rein and take a breather by just loping along. When you are ready to put him back into the exercises, stop him, put him back into the workout.

Move the shoulder

The walk

If you are just beginning these exercises, before you begin you will need to know how to move your horses body parts. These manoeuvres should be taught individually.

You will start with a walk turning that walk into a shoulder exercise by counter arching or bending.

- Walk in a left circle, as you walk, reach down with your right hand to take the rein, bring your hand now toward your bellybutton until you can see your horses' right eye.
- Still walking take your left rein and hold it off your horses' neck using your hand as a guide to move the shoulder to the left (remember your indicator hand in the serpentines)?
- With your right leg at the girth, squeeze your leg as if you were pushing him over to the left. Try pushing that right leg over the left leg, you probably won't make it at first but that

is what you are going to be striving for. You want your horse to move his right leg to the left, when you start doing this exercise around his hind end you will be looking to lift that leg over the left leg.

Once you have moved the shoulder around while walking a circle in an arc and you are comfortable that you and your horse are ready for the next stage, you can begin moving the shoulder around his hind end while you hold the arc that you started with.

Moving the shoulder around the stationary hindquarters

As you walk your horse, begin to slow him to a halt. Move his front right over his left front. He will probably take a step here and there with his hind, don't worry too much about it as long as your horse is crossing over in the front.

Use your right leg at the girth, push with your right leg until your horse lifts that leg and takes it across his chest and in front of his left leg.

Remember, it is terrific that you have accomplished this however, you want more than just the leg moving across from the elbow, strive to get that leg up and over coming out of the shoulder.

Stay on the same side until you feel your horse has mastered all the movements then change over and do the opposite side.

*Note: If you are arcing your horse using your right rein, you are working on the **right** lead leg and if arcing your horse using your left rein you are working on the **left** lead leg. So, if you were having trouble with your left lead and you wanted to work on it you would choose to pick up your left rein concentrating on that left lead leg (his working leg) as you cross his left leg over the right.*

Moving the hip

Your horse must move off your leg. There needs to be a basic understanding, with no questions asked, that your horse yield away from your leg every time you ask. This begins with a simple "leg yield" with your horse slightly counter bent. That means if you're stepping sideways to the left you can see the corner of his right eye. This is what we want to see in these four flowing manoeuvres, however, moving the hip doesn't necessarily mean you hold an arc. Sometimes, you want to move your horse's hip with less counter bend or more straightness. For these workout exercises though I like the counter arc/bend.

Does your horse move off your leg without the use of spurs? If so, that's great. If not, spurs could become a useful tool to help you to be more exact and precise with your aids. With your horse moving off your leg, begin to ask specifically for him to move his hip over. Start this at the standstill. Move your leg back and in asking your horse to move his hip over one step. You want him to keep his front end in one place.

Moving the hip while holding the horse's face in the same position as when moving the shoulder is definitely a more advanced exercise. When starting off a green broke or a horse that has never attempted these moves, I like to hold their face in the **opposite** direction to their hip being moved.

It may not sound like it when you first read the next points but it's easier to teach a green horse this way:

Example –

- Have your horse's head held to the **left**,
- Using your **left** leg behind the girth, push his hip to the **right**, this will move his hip around his front end with ease.
- When you are ready to teach the advanced move on the green broke and shape up for the lope transition to the **right**, stop and while standing still take note – head to the **left**, hip to the **right**. When you have that in your head, keep your left leg holding your horse's hip to the right and bump your **right rein** until your horse brings

his head around to the **right** – now your horse is shaped in the **right arc** ready to lope off on the **right** lead.

I know this sounds "mammoth" and you will definitely have to re-read the above points to get it to sink in. When you get it down pat it will be second nature. Training horse's is not meant to be too easy. Challenge yourself with these exercises they really are amazing at improving your horse's movement and mind.

When bringing the horse's face around to the right, you need to hold your left rein but not as firm, still taking more of your right rein than left but do take up the slack on the left rein here, you don't want to do this exercise on a loose rein, the draw reins are designed to help you without undue pressure on your horse's face.

At this stage, you are doing these body parts individually for now. When you and your horse are up to it you will advance to blending these exercises into one move which will be an advanced manoeuvre, train your horse well on the individual body parts before moving him up into the advanced moves.

If you combine the shoulder and hip, you will find that it sets you up for the lope transition very nicely you are ready to lope off on the right lead. You will be set in a soft arc to the right. Remember to also incorporate the back-up and side-pass in your workout, use the shoulder/hip combo for when you want to work on the lope transition.

Hang five on loping off

He is set for the lope transition. **BUT** you're not going to lope off, you're going to hold his frame like that and walk off for around 6 or 8 strides without changing a thing – using your **left** leg, holding his face slightly right. When you have walked him out a few strides, go back into "move the shoulder – move the hip", hold that frame walk off again. This is getting you and your horse ready for the **right** lead lope transition. When you feel that your horse is flowing from shoulder to hip and he is able to hold that frame when he walks off, bump it up to jogging off then from the jog you will be able to kiss your horse up into the lope, lope out of the manoeuvre and give your horse a break by loping in a few serpentines.

By now, your horse should have a bit of an idea on how to position his body for you, if you have been repetitive at these workout manoeuvres, he should be flowing straight into the manoeuvre's and be quite supple.

I find the more you loosen the reins, the more he's going to flounder around, either walk or jog step off *"like tomorrow will do"* before he eventually lopes off.

Once you have brought your horses face around slightly, DO NOT soften the grip, you need to lope off like that. Holding your horses frame in this position believe it or not is going to make it easier for him in the long run.

Hold, kiss, use your left leg/spur to ask for the lope. In a perfect world, you should get a sensational lope transition with him framed up, not with his head in the air hollowing out his back and trotting into a big old canter but a lovely, smooth, lifted transition.

It seems like a lot of hard work just to get a good lope transition, but I would rather put the work in and get a smooth, soft transition – if you get your transitions perfect, what follows will be perfect also.

Break it up for as long as you need to, don't be in a hurry to blend it all together in case it confuses you or your horse. Take your time as it is not a waste of time, teaching any one of these body parts will be an improvement even if you are not keen on blending the manoeuvres together.

Flowing all of these moves together in one workout move would look like this – Move the shoulder around in 2 or 3 full circles, remember not always the same number of turns, the same number of strides backing up, moving the hip and side-pass and not always in the same sequence. Flow from the shoulder to the backup from the back up to the hip, from the hip to the side-pass, from the side-pass to the shoulder. Mix them up and continue doing this workout for 10 minutes at the very least.

That key word … Repetition!

Remember repetition. Once you have gone through the workout, do it over and over again in that same lesson. When you feel your horse is doing his moves quite well – Reward, (don't go overboard with reward), a pat on the neck will suffice.

If you feel your horse is NOT putting in an effort, well there is another "R" word I use and that's Reprimand!!!!!!

Now hold on, before you drop your jaw to the ground, I have a reprimand for everything.

My reprimand is…**NO REWARD!**

Instead of a buddy pat on the neck, I go for the repetition deal. Sometimes, depending on the horse, they just don't finish on a good note for you to reward them and you can't stay out there all night waiting until you get a good move.

I zone in on an *"I tried hard"* move. Even if it's not picture-perfect, if you don't throw a reward in there somewhere, they won't get the gist of it really well.

Youngsters, they are the best, even if they get it wrong, I wait for the slightest "try" in them, I'll give them a pat and quit them. The next day, they always put a smile on my face because they come out into the arena dying to show me how good they are, then they keep on showing me even when I am not asking for anything!

The first few times especially if the horse is having trouble taking the lesson in, I will stick to the one side. Horses can become very confused if you change from one side to the other too quickly if they haven't got it down pat. Once they do get it, you can go ahead and change lead legs whenever it takes your fancy. I am mainly referring to a young, green horse when I say this. The older ones can probably cope with left to right, right to left pretty easily.

The back

Backing your horse is one of the manoeuvre's in this workout. Making sure you back your horse meaningfully, don't pull him back a couple of steps and stop. Remember, when you blend everything together it is going to be in one movement. The punishment fits the crime, if your horse is refusing to back or stops after he has backed two strides, back him further.

With both hands pull back evenly to get your horses feet moving, don't fuss where his head carriage is, you may find he will have his head fairly high, at this stage it doesn't matter where he is carrying his head, the main thing is he is moving his feet backward.

Back your horse 10 steps there-about. While teaching a young horse, you may only get five steps initially, work on getting more every day. Once you have backed your horse, move him into a different body part.

The side-pass?

Side-passing into the jog will clean up how your horse jogs off. Rather than dribbling along getting faster at the walk before they step into the jog, the side pass will have him jogging off from the walk in a natural and smooth transition. Careful, it can be classed as a break-of-gait when you are under the eye of the judge when your horse picks up speed at the walk to go up into the jog. It's a good thing I'm not a judge because if there is one thing (well there is more than one), I hate to see, is a horse that when asked to jog moving up from the walk gets faster and faster in the walk until they finally take that step into the jog – pet hate! Even if you strike it lucky and the judge doesn't see your sloppy transition, if it's not corrected this will, without a doubt put your horse further on the forehand. When he dribbles into it, he is actually leaning on his forehand. You won't usually see a horse that is balanced and off of his forehand dribble into a jog, he will click on up into the jog very easily and graciously.

When doing the side-pass in your workout with the four body parts you can give this a try. Put your horse in the side-pass and jog out of it to see how it cleans the transition into the jog up.

If you are simply working on your side-pass you can walk your horse off in a straight line for a little way. When you are ready, side pass to the left. Using both reins, have contact with your horse's mouth, even though you are moving side-ways, keep your horse straight this time from head to tail. While you have him side-passing start bumping him with both legs while still guiding him into the side-pass. Cue him with a cluck to put him into a jog whilst you are in the side-pass. Jog in a few serpentines before reversing directions and repeat to the right.

I also use this on an older horse that has been inadvertently let to do just that…dribble into the jog. It's not about the gait with this lesson it's about getting the horse to do a clean transition.

I like to side pass my horse when I have been sitting still chewing the fat with other riders, when I'm ready to move off and my horse isn't, side-passing to move off gets him back off his front end while he was having his five minutes unofficial snooze. It works really well in lifting the front end. It only needs two or three steps.

Two Tracking

When a horse is two tracking (also called Leg Yield) his body moves straight ahead, however, he will be tracking at a 45° degree angle across the arena.

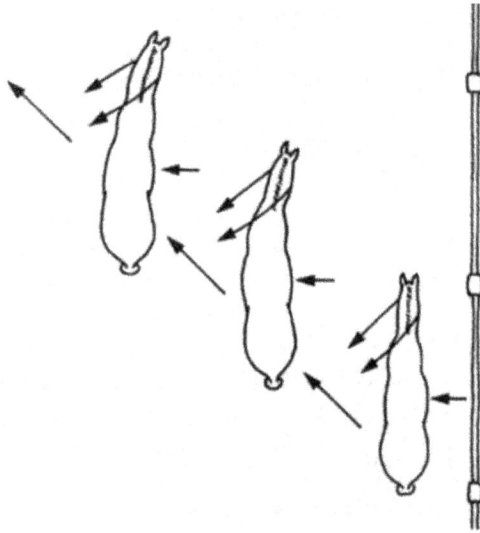

Two-track left.

It's similar to the "Half Pass". It's a lateral movement in which the horse moves forward and sideways at the same time. The difference between the two of them is the half pass requires more balance, engagement and collection from a horse than the Two Track. This is because the horse is slightly bent in the direction of movement in the Half Pass. In the Two Track, the horse is fairly straight or looking slightly away from the direction of travel.

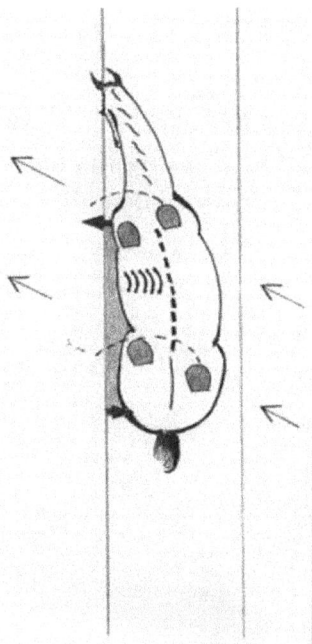

Half Pass facing in direction of travel

You will find, if you don't place your horse's head to the right with your hands, he will place it there himself because it's the easy way out for him. He doesn't need to try really hard when his head is facing in the opposite direction as to where he is travelling. Doing this, he will tend to drop that shoulder.

If you were to track left, you need to use the right leg to push the hindquarters to the left. It is really easy for the rider to 'lean' to the right while doing this, however, you have got to think straight. You need to sit *evenly* in the centre of your saddle, don't lean forward as this will put undue weight over your horse's front end and make it extremely difficult for your horse to do the manoeuvre.

Use both the direct (left) and the right rein, this will push the horse's shoulder slightly to the left.

At first, your horse's head will be bent to the right, I don't try to correct this as it is hard for them to learn to move their body over and complete it with a straight line initially, but as he responds more easily to your leg aid his head will come around more in the direction of travel.

Optimally, you want his body straight while doing this exercise so keep a timer on him having his head slightly to the right (or left depending on your direction). Whilst his head is to the right, he is dropping his left shoulder but you have got to start with baby steps so you know his left shoulder will be dropping but because you are on the ball, you are going to create a mistake to get what you want, then you will come back in and fix that turning head and get him straightened up again.

The Lope

How your horse handles his transitions will directly affect his gait. If he surges off into the trot or lope, he will stay faster than if he softly steps off into it. When moving forward from the walk or the jog, if he is "up" with lift and self-carriage, he should be able to lift up and lope right off, leaning into it or taking big long steps into the trot before he lopes off is not attractive at all and is not a true lope off transition. If he starts off incorrectly, then stop him and try again.

When asking a horse to step off correctly into the lope, he should move over off your outside leg and you should be able to control the step all the way into the lope. If I am choosing to lope off to the left, I want control of my horse's hip with my right leg. I will also hold his face slightly to the left as well putting him in that arc, while holding his face I will ask for the lope transition with my right leg on behind the girth. I want him to lift straight up into the lope from the walk (or jog) collected. If my horse rushes through my leg or tells me he is sensitive to my leg pressure I won't continue with it.

I stop what I am doing and will throw my horse into a calisthenic workout until I get his mind and body back to me. If I have one that is super flighty off my spur, I might hold my right leg on him. I will turn his head to the right and I will hold my right leg on making sure my spur is on him also. I will push his hip over then release my leg once he moves off of my leg, I will keep repeating this several times making sure I do not release his face. I will hold his face around to the one side and use my leg on that same side, leg goes on and off, his face stays where I have put it until he accepts my leg/spur.

If you perfect your transitions smooth and calm, you will perfect your gaits. Your lope actually starts from the transition, if that's not right your lope will deteriorate more and more as you keep loping.

When it comes to the lope, I think many people are confused about how much importance to place upon slow. I believe it is more important for your horse to move *correctly* first. If you ride a horse that is 16 hands it shouldn't be expected of him to be able to hold the same speed as a horse that is 14.3 hands. Loss of forward momentum resulting in an animated and/or artificial gait at the lope won't see you in the winner's circle, the animated, artificial gait should be scored as a fault according to how severe it is.

The Rule book will tell you – The horse should be ridden at a speed which is a **natural way of going**. The head should be carried at an angle which is natural and suitable to the horse's conformation at all gaits.

I like to push my horses out a touch in the early stages of training, enough that they can maintain a cadenced and balanced lope. Not only does this work in my favour down the track with speed control, my horses will also show presence in their expression, working with their ears forward and looking through the bridle like they are enjoying what they are doing.

Eventually, when my horse becomes accustomed with carrying my weight and can travel balanced, I will then start to think about slowing everything down. I will also do the same with the older horse that has come to me for training, they may have been forced into slow from the get go, if this is the case, he may not have a very good way of moving, he may trope or bob, he may have excessive knee action. All of these faults can be manmade because the rider is in a hurry to have their horse going slow. Get correct movement before slow movement.

A horse needs to possess a good, deep drive from behind and lift in front to enable him to stay slow. Lift is very important to maintaining self-carriage at a slower speed. A horse with a strong drive allows them to reach up underneath themselves. A horse that can drive from behind and lift in front with every stride will display a moment of suspension in their lope gait which will slow down the rhythm and the stride in a more natural manner.

A horse travels naturally at the lope when in a slight arc. Don't mistake this for over canting which is a term used when a horse has overshot with his outside hind leg, placing it too far to the inside, giving the impression that he is "crabbing" down the rail...picture how a crab moves. Some riders do this because it slows the horses forward motion down.

The maximum arc a horse should display is if he was in a left lead lope, his right hind leg will be in between the two front legs and a fraction of his left eye will be visible to you. If he was loping on the right lead, his left rear would be in between the two front legs you would see a fraction of his right eye. Keeping the horse in the correct arc every step of the way is what you need to strive for.

I cannot see the beauty in this way of going when the horse's outside hind is further to the inside of the arena than the horse's inside front foot…It is not natural!

Your workout exercises are what will get and keep your horse in the correct arc. Your training of gaining control of all of your horse's body parts. If your horse is under-arcing, you need to push his hindquarters off your leg to the inside.

Your horse is over arcing or over canting when their head is to the outside facing the rail and the hindquarters are over-canted into the inside, he will be crabbing down the rail. He is not following his nose and his shoulders are not square going down the rail. Try bringing his nose to the inside and drive him up into the bit at the walk or the jog by lifting your reins and bumping or sacking out your legs on his sides. Go back to the lope on the rail, keeping his shoulders facing square down the rail following his nose in the direction you are going. If he loses position or over arcs, I like to fix this by loping down the rail on the wrong lead and placing my *inside* leg behind the girth and squeeze his hind quarters over a touch toward the rail or the outside to take a little of that overexaggerated arc from him. Because he is on the rail, he can't push his hindquarters over too far as the rail will block this from happening. You will need to soften up on your outside or rail leg when you do this. When you feel your horse straighten up in his body, release your inside leg slightly ready to repeat if he starts over canting again but keep loping down the rail in the same direction.

Some older more seasoned horses will push their hip over too much to the inside, sometimes down the rail one way or the other, I've never had one that over canted both ways but I assume they are out there somewhere. I make it a point to do this counter canter exercise with them every day and for a good half hour.

Be aware of what shape the front end is in. If you haven't kept up with your exercises on the front end, keeping your horse up in the shoulders, he will be quicker and heavier. He should be carrying more of his body weight on his back end, not up front. Carrying his weight on his front end is also known as being "downhill".

If I am at a show, I like to get their shoulders up and get them light with as little disturbance to the other horse's and rider's as possible. When I feel the horse getting heavy on the front end or getting faster, I will stop and back three or four strides, do a rollback and lope off in the other direction. I like to make sure that when I am doing these rollbacks, I turn in toward the rail some of the time as this will help tighten them up. They have to suck back a tad more when facing the rail.

Always be mindful of your horse's front end, as soon as he feels heavier or starts to quicken up, repeat the sequence of stopping, backing and roll back. The more you do this exercise, the further distance he will get holding himself in the correct frame. You will definitely feel it when they are lighter up front. The main purpose is to redirect body weight back over the hindquarters and increase your horse's self-discipline to carry himself for longer periods of time.

When checking my horses balance, I will take my work out to the centre of the pen I will pick a mark on the back wall, drape my reins and walk my horse toward the mark that I have picked out on the wall. If my horse veers off to either side tells me he is not travelling balanced. If he can lean to one side or the other, he can also lean forward on his front end.

If my horse drifts off either way or leans forward I will stop and turn him in the opposite direction that he was leaning in, depending on the severity, I may do a full 360 and continue on or I will turn and continue in the opposite direction draping my rein I will test his straightness again, if he is leaning in any direction, I will correct him by turning him in the opposite direction and repeat the process.

Riding on a loose rein

Riding on a loose rein comes from training self-carriage. Self-carriage is your horse's ability to properly carry himself on his own. Your horse needs to be able to carry himself in "self-carriage" and not rely on you to continuously hold him up in the correct frame with your hands and your legs. Sure, we can help them by keeping our legs on in a comfortable position ready to use them at any time we need to. I never take my legs off, if I'm riding, my legs are on, they may be light and soft but they are still on.

When your horse has been trained to have self-carriage, he's going to naturally be able to hold his shoulders up while being able to maintain a rounded back which will demonstrate true self carriage and maintain collection on his own.

Not allowing his shoulders to sink down so that his back hollows out and he drops his weight onto his front end.

Why do you need this?

Western pleasure is often looked at as being an easy class to compete in however, it's not as easy as it seems. Western pleasure is difficult not only because it must be done on a loose rein, but it's also performed at a slower speed, giving the impression to the judge and spectators that there is very little assistance needed by the rider, it's imperative that your horse has the training and discipline to hold himself in a balanced frame while performing the walk, jog, and lope in a collected manner.

How this all comes about is to firstly achieve collection by holding your horse's face and applying pressure with your legs, which will encourage him to lift in front, round his back and drive from his hindquarters. This is "driving into the bit", it is also known as riding through your hands. Secondly, the next step is to create enough 'hold' or 'stay' that you can show him in the class on a loose rein.

Horses are athletes, when trained to carry themselves in a position where they are rounded and lifting their shoulders, the hindquarters now will naturally drive through, it will become second nature to them to balance and collect at a slower, cadenced and balanced gait.

It is necessary to train your horse to have self-carriage throughout his show career, it's something that needs to be carried out in his daily training. Every time you take your horse out for training you should first, warm them up, you can do this with lunging your horse or you can long trot in some figure eights. Once you have warmed your horse up you should get back in to your workout routine daily. It is a life-long thing that you have to keep up with.

It's a good idea if you can develop "feel" in your legs, hands and seat and it is most helpful if you understand what you are feeling under you is right or wrong and you know when and how to fix it. If you have read the section on the workout routine in this book, you will understand that it's not about pulling on the reins to get a slow, cadenced horse.

If your horse is continuing to speed up and get out of frame, go back to your workouts, – move the shoulder, move the hip, side-pass and backup. Not always in that order but give him a good work out. Then when you are riding out of those exercises and he speeds up don't be in a hurry to go for the reins, use your seat and your legs. The punishment fits the crime, if he continues to speed up when you get out of the exercises you have to put him back into the exercises. Do four or five shoulder and hip exercises, side pass them for a good distance and back them just as far. If you do this immediately, they speed up, they will work it out that these workouts are like a reprimand for speeding up, he will get it and want to slow his pace. Don't slow him down with your reins, go with your leg aids first. Don't rely on your reins for speed control.

If you are repetitive with your workout routine exercises, he will definitely want to go slow. You have to throw him into the routine as soon as he mucks up. You then have to drape your reins and let him lope off on a drape (or jog or walk). You have to give him the benefit of the doubt – trust him – fix him if he mucks up even if you have to do this sequence of exercises one hundred times, do it 101 times, he will learn to carry himself in the correct frame which in turn will make him slow down. The more balanced you have him by doing the exercise routine, the slower he will be able to travel correctly.

"Perfect practice makes practice perfect".

Don't overkill on the slowness Western pleasure is not all about how slow you can go especially if it's sacrificing correct movement, cadence and balance. It's more important to exhibit true gaits than it is to compromise the quality of movement.

Remember your workouts?

If you are having some problems with your horse not wanting to slow and travel in a relaxed, collected manner, teaching your horse to lope on a draped rein is as simple as going back to your workouts. Do your workout exercises before you begin any other task, if they lose frame, speed up or do something wrong, throw them straight into the workout exercises. Use them not only as a fix but for a reprimand. There is absolutely no hope at getting your horse to slow down and travel on a drape if there is a continuous pull on the reins. The horse will slow while you are holding their face but when you let go, he is going to speed back up again.

According to the Rule Book – here is how our horse should be travelling...

The Walk

The walk is a natural, flat-footed, four-beat gait. The horse must move straight and true at the walk. The walk must be alert, **with a stride of reasonable length in keeping with the size of the horse**.

Poor walk – uneven pace and no cadence. Has no flow and may appear intimidated or appear to march.

Average walk – has a four-beat gait, level top-line and is relaxed.

Good walk – has a flowing four-beat gait, level top-line, relaxed and is bright and attentive.

The Jog

The jog is a smooth, ground-covering two-beat diagonal gait. The horse works from one pair of diagonals to the other pair. The jog should be square, balanced and with straight, forward movement of the feet. Horses walking with their back feet and trotting in the front are not considered performing the required gait.

Unacceptable jog. Cannot perform a two-beat gait and has no flow or balance in the motion. Poor jog: hesitates in motion. Does not keep an even and balanced motion or a level top-line and may appear to shuffle. Slightly below average jog: average motion but has negative characteristics such as: walking with hind legs, dragging the rear toes or taking an uneven length in stride with the front and rear legs.

Correct or average jog: has a two-beat gait, a level top line and a relaxed appearance.

Good jog: has an average motion with positive characteristics such as balance and self-carriage while taking the same length of strides with the front and rear legs.

Very good jog: is comfortable to ride while having a consistent two-beat gait. The horse guides well, appears relaxed and has a level top-line.

Excellent jog: effortless and very efficient motion. Swings the legs yet touches the ground softly. Confident, yet soft with its motion while being balanced and under control. Moves flat with the knee and hock and have some cushion in the pastern. Has a bright and alert expression and exhibits more lift and self-carriage than the "very good jog".

Extended Jog: When asked to extend the jog, it moves out with the same smooth way of going as in the jog.

Poor extended jog: never lengthen the stride and may appear rough to ride.

Average extended jog: moves up in its pace and appears smooth to ride.

Good extended jog: has an obvious lengthening of stride with a slight increase in pace while exerting less effort and appears smooth to ride.

The Lope

The lope is an easy, rhythmical, forward moving three-beat gait. Horses moving to the left should lope on the left lead. Horses moving to the right should lope on the right lead. The horse should lope with a **natural stride** and appear relaxed and smooth.

Unacceptable lope: does not have a three-beat gait. Has no flow, rhythm or balance. Uncomfortable ride. Horses travelling at a four-beat gait are not considered to be performing at a proper lope.

Poor lope: appears to have a three-beat lope but has no lift or self-carriage. The horse shuffles, has no flow and bobs his head, giving the appearance of exerting a great deal of effort to perform the gait. Also, could be uncomfortable to ride.

Slightly below average lope: has an average motion but exhibits negative characteristics like head bobbing, not completing the stride with the front leg and leaving the outside hock well behind the horse's buttocks.

Average lope: has a true three-beat gait with a level top-line and very little head and neck motion. He is relatively straight (not over-canted); guides well and has a relaxed appearance.

Good lope: has an average motion but exhibits positive characteristics in his performance like self-carriage, a steady top-line, relaxed appearance and is responsive to the rider's aids.

Very good lope: has more lift and flow than the average horse. Has a strong but smooth drive from behind. He may bend his knee slightly yet still has a level top-line while exhibiting self-carriage with a relaxed appearance. Appears comfortable to ride.

Excellent lope: has a round back with an effortless strong, deep stride with the rear legs and a flat swing with the front legs. He keeps a level top-line, a relaxed yet alert and confident appearance and correct but soft in appearance. A special horse with a great lift and self-carriage.

Add in a bit of camouflage

Weighted reins are truly fabulous to ride with. I had many pairs of weighted reins, one set for each bridle. Weighted reins have such a good balance to them, they hold a beautiful drape and they don't swing like the lighter reins do.

Tip: If you ride a horse that tends to roc up front such as a head bobber, a set of weighted reins will help disguise this a little. Weighted reins are just that, weighted, they are weighted in the right places. Being weighted, they don't swing around as much as a lighter pair of reins and won't distract the judge as much.

A weighted rein refers to a rein that is heavier on one or both ends. Naturally weighted reins are cut from hides that are specifically chosen for their weights and thicknesses. No extra leather or additional materials are added to them.

To cut good bridle reins only very good hides can be used. The hides are laid out flat and the reins are cut across the entire length of each hide with the thicker, heavier areas of the hides becoming the tail and bit ends of the reins. The heavy neck end of the hide that becomes the tails of the reins balances out the slightly less heavy but longer butt end of the hide which becomes the bit ends. This gives the bridle reins balance in your hands and a nice drape.

Does your horse cut corners?

Unfortunately, any horse has the potential to become a corner cutter. It is one of those niggling issues, that if it is not addressed correctly once and for all with correct training, it will plague almost all activities you choose to do with your horse.

If you are not on the ball when approaching your corners your horse will soon learn to shave a bit off here and shave a bit off there until you will find that you are not doing your corners at all. This will cause your horse to not only drop his inside shoulder, he will start to speed up and lose all cadence along the long side of the rail, gaining a bit more speed at every corner cut.

If your horse is long and 'strung out', he will not be able to ride deep into the corner, which may in turn make your circles and corners look similar! This is where he will drop into the centre more with his inside shoulder and gain momentum.

You need to ensure you have your horse responsive to your cues with your legs to be able to ask for slightly more drive and more collection when approaching the corner, you want to be able to have your horse know your inside leg so that you can keep him where you want him and drive him up through the corner at the same time. Have the confidence that he won't push through your inside leg and drop in.

Train them into the corners

There is an exercise I really love to do that works wonders at correcting your horse and getting them in the corners as much as possible.

I love it because it kills more than one bird with that stone! Not only are you working on cleaning up your corners but you are working on…

- "Naturally" slowing your horse down rather than "artificially" cranking him down and forcing the slow on him.
- Keeps his shoulders up
- Elongates the front lead leg. As he travels around the corner, he will naturally want to reach out with his lead leg
- Helps keep a compact, tight frame rather than flattening out and hollowing out his top line.

After all, Western Pleasure is a rail event so we want to be able to show our horses off on the rail in this class and that includes the corners.

Squares

I like to take my horse into the centre of the arena for this, I begin at the walk riding four straight lines and four corners. As you come into each corner ask for a half halt use both legs on the horse to create impulsion from behind. (Going to the left in this example).

Close your fingers around both reins make sure you don't pull your hands back to your body as you will just shorten the horse's neck rather than achieving connection. With the outside rein create an "honest" contact. Create ever so slight inside bend by applying a little more pressure with the inside leg, at the same time using the outside leg to stop the horse swinging its hind quarters.

Use 'sponge fingers' squeeze and release as though you were squeezing water out of a sponge with the inside hand to keep the neck straight. Hold what would feel like a half halt (asking the horse to prepare to **halt** in balance, before pushing it onward to continue in its gait.) or, as I like to call it – *ride through the brake,* for the two or three seconds that you're travelling through the turn, and then release the pressure of the half halt and ride the horse forward onto the straight line.

Whether you're on a turn or a straight line, remain aware of the horse's position beneath you. The horse's shoulders should remain square in front of the rider's shoulders at all times. Common mistakes are for the horse to fall out through his outside shoulder on the turn, or swing his quarters. Over steering your horse with your left rein around the corner can also see him dropping or leaning around the corner. If you don't keep a check on your own body position, this can also cause your horse to lean or cut. Make sure you are centered in the saddle, keep checking your position to make sure you are not leaning to the inside of the corner yourself, this will surely have your horse following your path. Stay centered and square in your own body.

Keep things simple by remembering that each hand and leg controls its respective quarter of the horse. If he falls out through the shoulder create more weight in the outside rein and if he swings his quarters out use the outside leg slightly further back to stop that. Remember that this is quite hard work for the horse so take a break from the exercise before he gets tired.

After coming out of a corner, give him a loose rein. I would normally do no more than five or six corners in a row on a young horse.

The Trot

Once you have got the idea, trot the square before you attempt the square at the jog. This tends to be easier on a green horse. It also encourages them to keep their hind end up and under themselves. Keeping them from learning bad habits such as dragging their hind end behind them while pulling the front end along.

As you bring them up to the trot, make your straight lines a little longer.

Trotting up to the corner – The same principle applies – squeeze your legs and seat, make contact with the face and hold that as you get his shoulder around the corner, holding his inside shoulder up with your inside leg.

Straighten up as soon as you come out of the corner and ride him at the trot to your next corner.

Note – Try and sit to the trot, don't post. Raise your hands up, keeping your elbows at your side. Bending at the elbows and keeping your hands about 8 or 10 inches apart bring them up NOT BACK BEHIND YOUR HIPS!

The Lope

Begin loping on your straight line, when you approach your first corner squeeze your legs, get heavier in your seat and lift your hands at the same time, rounding the horse underneath you by driving him up into the bit, framing them up, preparing them for the corner.

Do your corner in the same way, lift, hold and feel that half halt or ride through the break around the corner.

Remember not to "steer" them around the corner with your left rein, keep your hands close in a mirror fashion with each other at about 8 to 10 inches apart and at about your chest height.

It's a "collection" around the corner keeping everything tight and clean.

You can continue on with this exercise quite easily every day as a refresher.

This exercise will help you and your horse approach the corners of the arena with more balance and cadence. Your horse should be able to ride up into a corner with your leg aids that you used when you rode the square enabling you to drape your reins.

SVQ Cashed Up and David Pearce

– Give them an inch...

It's good to give your horse a chance to prove himself. Testing your horse on a draped or loose rein while approaching the corners is something you should do.

I actually *want* them to make the mistake of trying to cut the corner. This is why I like to drape my reins and test him out, waiting for him to drift off the rail. This gives the rider another chance at setting in concrete the exercises of the square. The more times a horse chooses to make a mistake, the more times a rider has to perfect the manoeuvre.

After all, this is why I am spending time on correcting this bad habit in the first place. A horse will always try and do what is most comfortable for them, they like to find an easy way out.

If my horse does try and take the easy way out and cut the corner, I will lift my reins, holding my **outside rein** soft, my inside rein is going to be a block as well as keeping his shoulder up. I will stop then ask for a side-pass deep into that corner, once in there, I will stop and sit for a few seconds to let him take that in. I will drop my reins and walk out of the corner.

I will do this at all three gaits, if and when they cut the corner, I will lift the reins, stop, go through everything I did at the walk. I will wait in the corner then I will jog out NOT allowing him to take a few long, strided walk steps I WILL JOG OUT. If I am loping, I will do exactly the same up until the halt in the corner for a few seconds then I will frame him up for the lope transition and I want him to lope out of the corner.

Side-passing my horse into the corner is my reprimand for cutting it. I make sure that when I have him back on the rail he is able to stand for a bit and take it in before I ask him to continue along the rail.

Don't go slow to get slow!

Sounds wrong…right?

Try getting your horse to slow down in a more natural way rather than forcing them. If they are forced to lope slow it will tear their leg movement up, they won't look natural and certainly won't enjoy their job.

Below, is just one way of Teaching your horse to lope slow…

Back in the day, when I was just starting out, before I had a mobile phone in my back pocket. I had this outside filly that I was working on training her up for western pleasure, she was a 2-year-old Chicks Impressive Charm bred filly.

Everything was ticking along nicely until the day came when I wanted to turn the canter into a lope on this "green broke" filly.

No matter what exercise I tried to slow her down, she had one gear – flat out and that was all I was going to get.

This filly sure had me scratching my head, I was growing tired of it, she obviously wasn't.

Reverse Psychology

Have you ever used reverse psychology on a child or even an adult for that matter? I used it on this filly one day, I let her canter and canter and canter, I was along for the ride. Then finally, she started to slow down by herself, I pushed her on further saying to myself "no, you want to canter, let's canter".

I pushed her on every time I felt her come back which was probably another three large laps.

We came out again the next week, same thing – she wanted to power on so power on we did. This particular time as she slowed the first time, she slowed super, super slow on a draped rein. Rather than sit there and just go with her I put some leg on and gathered a bit of rein up, rounded her up a bit and just loped on around the circle for a lap.

From that day forward that filly just wanted to lope the house down with her slow lope. She went on to be a National Champion Youth Horse; State and NPHA level Champion before being exported to NZ where for many years was undefeated in Open, Amateur and Youth Western Pleasure, Hunter Under Saddle, Trail, Horsemanship and later on became a pretty darn good Reiner…
The path she nearly went down back in those "canter non-stop" circle days.

That was how I trained my horses to "naturally" slow down. *I polished it up a bit over the years with serpentine's and other manoeuvres.*

Not all horses are the same

This took me a week to get this on that particular horse, I have gone much longer on other's, the penny seemed to take so long to drop for some of them. Others, have clicked within a couple of days. I continually repeat –

"Horses are not round pegs going into round holes. They are very much individuals."

I've known people to take "training a horse" a certain way as Gospel and must be done that particular way.

No, it isn't, you have to learn to be flexible, be prepared to go take a break, think on it. Come up with another way around it. **Don't force that round peg into a square hole** it will come back to bite you on the bum one day.

Give this a go with patience, you may need plenty of it. If it's not working for you, try and approach it in a different way, there are other ways to get the go slow in the lope, this is just one way I like to try initially. Now days, I let them canter at their pace but I will do serpentines, this slows them down quicker, they don't seem to like turning here, there and everywhere while they are going fast.

You have to be patient. Keep in mind getting the go slow "*naturally*" without ripping up their legs, getting them climbing, leaving their hind end at the last corner. You get a much nicer "*slow*" when done as naturally as you can. Let them think it was their idea.

First few times on the rail

On a young horse that hasn't been introduced to the rail as yet or, an older horse that needs re-training, I like to use another trick of the trade that went into my tool box once I learnt it from my mentor and that is:

- Work your horse in the centre of the arena as usual. Use the calisthenic workout, get your horse warmed up and supple.
- After about a 15 to 20 minute workout in the middle, ride your horse over to the fence and "join" him to the fence on a gentle angle then stop and rest for a bit. Let your horse have a breather, let him relax.
- Continue along the rail at the walk to begin with for a distance.
- Bring your horse off the rail and put him back into calisthenics.
- Repeat the above manoeuvres several times and on a daily basis.

When you're ready, begin to bring your horse over to the rail at the jog. There will be a slight difference, this time you will jog to the rail, you won't stop when you get to the rail, continue on at the jog along the rail then stop. Repeat the process. Remembering to give your horse a workout in the middle of the arena before returning to the rail. Working out in the centre doesn't have to be for too long a period, just enough that you can teach your horse the difference from the centre of the pen to the rail.

Loping over to the rail on a soft angle, don't head to it straight on, approach the rail on a soft angle and keep on loping down the rail before you stop for a breather – repeat the process.

Again, you will be creating a problem when you do this. The problem here is that when your horse finds out how good it is on the rail, that it's a great place to be, he won't want to leave! Read the next chapter for fixing this.

Once they learn to enjoy the rail, I will find that I no longer need to be showing my horse the rail this way every day once they hook on. Then you need to get them to hook off too, they tend to want to stay on the rail, they figure out they have to work out in the centre.

Overtaking – getting back on the rail

Whatever the reason for drifting on or off the rail, the fix is the same.

This is similar to getting your horse to stop cutting corners

You will have read how I allow my horse to make the mistake – trying to cut the corner so that I can correct him.

I remember one particular horse that developed this habit of not wanting off the rail *and then* leaking into the centre nearing the end of the class. Her name was Irrizippable, (Blue Denim Zipper). She was a fabulous horse, so very talented. I swear, she knew her place was in the arena.

We would be warming up in the warm up pen, the in-gate was a Gate Marshall with a rope. "Nikki" would watch that gate like a hawk, waiting for it to open. Even then, there was no stopping her, she wanted in that pen, it was all I could do to stop her from going in too early!

She was so smart, she began to listen to the announcer and even jump the gun on him too, she would anticipate the gaits, the turn-arounds, walk into the centre – everything, but, she was still hard to beat!

I had to really be on the ball with her, I had to anticipate not *if* but *when* she was going to make her moves. But it was even more than that, Nikki also loved being on the rail. If we were in behind a slower horse and I needed to get off the rail to overtake and re-gain a good position back on the rail…what a task that was!

She was either wanting to hug the rail or anticipate the end of the class, leaking in to get to the middle of the pen for presentation.

It was a good thing she was winning almost every time she went into the pen!

This is what I did

When you train on your own every day at home, you have to get creative because tying horses up around the rail so that I could practice coming off the rail around them in my arena was out of the question, I wasn't prepared to destroy the footing of my arena with horses pawing and digging giant holes to try fix this problem.

Next best thing – put a bath tub on the rail, of course! It's not something everyone needs to do by the way, I chose a tub because it was what I had on hand. You could even recruit your friends. Get them to come and ride with you in your arena, or theirs. Have them go slow on the rail and you can practice going around them.

I put my horse on the rail at the walk to begin with. As I approached the tub, I would cue her to leave the rail by putting my outside leg on her and laying the outside rein on her neck (one handed, bridled up). She had to come off the rail or run into the bath, however, on the other side of the tub, she was moving back in onto the rail on her own virtually as soon as she was just past the bath tub.

I couldn't have her doing this because if she did this at a show on top of the horse she just past it would be disastrous – It happened one time, the horse she past was a stallion too, not a good thing! I had to rectify this pretty quick.

I let her take two or three strides toward the rail, making sure she knew my outside leg and rein were definitely on her to discourage her from going there, I wanted her to know that I wasn't just along for the ride, I wanted her to *feel* my cues to correct her.

After about the third stride in toward the rail I ran my right hand down the inside rein so that there was equal pressure on both reins, cueing her with my legs and hands to stop, straight into a short backup of about 3 or 4 strides then straight into a side-pass *away* from the rail. Side-passing her until she was nearly to the other side of the arena before I would say whoa. I would then ease off, ride her back on to the closest part of the rail and continue on.

Repeating this every time she tried moving back on the rail through my hand and leg cue. I repeated this at all gaits.

After a few days, I took the tub out then I began to ride her on the rail one handed and wait for her to leak into the centre. Now being the horse that she was, she was in no hurry to leave the rail, she was happy to stay on the rail, especially at home with no announcer, crowds etc. and just walk around. This is where I had to "coax" her to leave the rail so that I could work on correcting her – even though she didn't leave the rail on her own accord.

To coax her I would lay my outside leg on her side and the outside rein at the same time, I would run my right hand down the inside rein and pull on it lightly until she came off the rail, letting go of the right rein (inside) immediately she took the bait, I would let her move in as if going into the centre. I would let her get to about 15 feet off the rail then I would bring that inside rein back into play holding it strong up against her neck enough that her head was now facing the middle of the pen and I would side-pass her briskly back to the rail. I would continue up along the rail at the side-pass a little way then drop out and walk on.

Again, repeating this scenario time and again until in the end, she was no way, no how, going to come off the rail until she was cued to come off by the proper cues from me.

I was actually *killing two birds with the one stone* in the one lesson. I was either cueing her to stay on the rail or cueing her to come off.

I did this daily at home with her and at all of the shows we went to. In the end I only had to check in on her once or twice trying to get her to leave the rail, she wasn't falling for it. In the end she started respecting my cues, if I wanted to overtake, she overtook and then waited for me to cue her when the time was right to get back on the rail.

The takeaway…

A horse will listen to your cues if they are done correctly and meaningfully, don't give your cues half-arsed, that's the time you will lose their respect for you.

A quote from Pat Parelli

"A horse doesn't care how much you know until he knows how much you care".

Repeat the scenario over and over on a daily basis. You don't necessarily need to go out and get a bath, I mean, this would work just like I was saying above, get your friends in etc. or don't use anything, I wanted an object so that the horse knew exactly what was required of her when she got to the tub.

In the end, your horse will respect you and wait on you as opposed to them taking over the situation.

Cheating on you

If your horse is cheating you by not staying on the rail, cutting corners, speeding up on the way back or refusing to go over an obstacle, you need to take a deeper look at your role. First, you must understand what the underlying motivations of the horse are and how you got to this point. Then you must figure out a plan for what's next, how you will change your horse's behaviour and change the way you ride.

Recognise the disobedience

If a horse has been properly trained and is a well-seasoned horse, this is not going to be a steering problem.

A horse that is leaking into the middle from the rail, cutting the corners, pulling toward the gate or stopping at the gate is disobedient to the aids of the rider. The first step in fixing this issue is to recognize it as disobedience.

Stopping your horse without picking up on the reins

Studying riders in the show pen, watching some of them as the announcer would call for the halt, I would feel myself cringe if I saw a rider using their reins excessively. If at all, your reins should only be used to halt with a squeeze of your fingers on the reins if you are riding two handed and the tweak of your pointing finger and ever so slight lift of your wrist if you are showing one handed.

There is nothing worse than seeing riders' pull their horses up like they were riding alongside John Wayne in a western movie. I love John (God Bless his soul), but you really don't want your halt cue to be *that* noticeable.

What about the "spur stop" deal?

Spur stop controversy

Seen in nearly all breeds, the spur stop requires a horse to perform with an extremely loose, draped rein at all times. Western pleasure horses have always travelled on a fairly loose rein, but in recent years the visible "drape" in the rein has become exaggerated. However, it requires time, good riding ability, and careful training to correctly teach a horse "self-carriage," particularly to slow or stop by responding to only a rider's use of seat position, upper leg and voice cues without tightening the reins. Thus, an alternative method of training to slow a horse down without the use of the reins gave rise to a new, highly controversial, technique known as the "spur stop," an unconventional method used by some trainers to train horses to slow down and stop when spur pressure is applied.

Because spur, heel or leg pressure is generally used to ask a horse to go faster, this technique is sometimes referred to by its critics as "riding the brake" and is frowned upon by several major western pleasure sanctioning organizations since at least 2003, when AQHA put out a series of videos on correct and incorrect style and way of going for western pleasure horses, showing a "hit list" of undesirable traits not to be rewarded in the show ring, with the spur stop leading the list.

This controversy in Western Pleasure circles resembles the debate over **Rollkur** in the field of **dressage**, particularly over the question of whether the practice constitutes animal abuse.

Mark Sheridan, an AQHA judge and trainer, has said:

"You should not have any problems with the spur stop, and the transition to whatever events you decide to do with [the horse]. Personally, I put a spur stop on just the stop and back, on my western riders."

A less extreme method is referred to as putting "buttons" on the horse. A "button" is simply a leg or spur position that tells the horse to travel at a particular gait or speed.

I will explain how and why I train my horses to listen to my spurs

Spurs are one more fine way to signal to your horse what you would like them to do. Spur stops are a very specific signal some western pleasure horses are trained to do.

At its core, spurs are not for "go," usually. Some trainers use them that way. However, my "go" is simply bumping my legs. Bumping, or "sacking my legs out on his sides" with my calves. If my horse doesn't respond to me bumping his sides with my calves, I will turn my toes in slightly so that the sides of my heels can bump the horse's sides along with my calves, and clucking to get him to move up into a jog. Most green broke horse's that yet need to learn the bumping cue go through this training with me, and some older horse's need to be trained on this if they have in the past been ridden with no leg on unless they had to be kicked up into the next gait.

Even with wearing my spurs I can use the insides of my heels to help bump the horse up. If I am still finding my horse is on another planet and not listening to my cues, I simply speed up my bumping rather than bang on his sides with my spurs.

Teaching a horse to come back and/or stop with a "spur stop"

There are a couple of different opinions on what a spur stop is. Some people claim

> 1.   Using a spur stop is to **ride** with your spur on keeping your horse from speeding up and to stop them.
>
> 2.   The spur stop is used to slow your horse's forward movement down and to cue to stop and back.

I personally would not go near number 1. This is exactly what I mean by causing a horse to "climb". I agree to why this way of riding is classed as abusive riding. If you rode your horse day in day out with your spur dug into his sides to ask him to go slow and to stop, I would like to bet that you would create a "climber" – The horse is artificially held back and finds itself with nowhere else to go but climb with its front end. He develops an over-exaggerated bend in his knee, it also blocks their engine which is their hind drive, freezing up the shoulders. Not to mention how uncomfortable it would be for your horse.

Other reasons why you don't want to be riding your horse this way is

> 1. Your horse will grow to become dull to your leg aids and spur cues because he gets no reward if your horse did slow down, if you don't take those spurs off and ease up on the legs, how will he know what you are asking of him?

2. You won't last five minutes if you ride your horse with your legs and spurs holding him from going forward, especially when he does get dull to them. You will have to become stronger in your leg then he will become dull to that, it will be a vicious cycle – you squeezing with all your might and your horse ignores it all.

3. Riding the "spur stop" totally tears your horse's leg movement up as mentioned above but it also has the horse hiding behind the bit and you don't want that.

How I developed my program

I can recall many a year ago, a friend of mine invited me to have a ride on her horse, I accepted, it wasn't until I wanted to stop that I hit a brick wall. My friend explained to me that I should sit deep in the saddle and put a lot of weight in my stirrups. Do you think I could do that! It was the most frustrating feeling, I truly could not reach with my feet at the same time as putting weight in my backside! When I tried, my back would round and my legs would go way too far forward for my liking. Talk about no co-ordination! I put it down to being too short for it but my friend shot me down in flames stating she was shorter than me.

I suppose it's what you get used to. Before I developed my way of riding with my seat and using my legs on the horse to slow them down, I was a member of the John Wayne club.

My method of using the "spur stop" is not to have my legs and spur on my horse from **go to whoa**. I teach them the spur stop, however, when I get that finesse, I don't need to use my spurs from go to whoa, I don't need to use the spur period, unless I need to go to plan B.

Plan B is when my horse isn't listening to my cues in the excitement of being in a big show pen with lots of other horses, people in the stands, different noises and smells. Only then, when he has zoned out is when I use the "spur stop," apart from that, my horse will come back to me when I squeeze with my butt and thighs, that's usually enough to get their attention. As long as I have done my training in a repetitive manner (daily), he will not need my spurs in his sides continuously.

I don't have to round my back, I am sitting up straight, my legs are in line with my body, close to my horse's sides and not thrust out in front of me.

Once my horse knows the spur stop, I fine tune my rein cues. The rein cues are also subtle, near on invisible and best of all on a drape.

Here's how I slow them down on a drape

I will set my horse up on one side of my arena – the long side. My intentions are to walk from one side of the arena to the other as slowly as possible. This intent may take days or it may take under an hour. The secret is just stick with it, don't leave anything out and it WILL work.

Sitting on my horse with a draped rein, I will relax my legs from the knee down I will begin to gently swing my legs toward and away only about 3 inches from the horse's girth in a sacking out manner, I ask him to walk on. Without touching my reins, I allow the horse to walk off. He will do this at *his* pace, I know it's not going to be slow and steady, but fast and loose. I have to let my horse make this move so that I can 'explain' with my legs that it is way too fast.

He begins his journey across the arena, sure enough, lightning fast. This is when I stop sacking him out with my legs, rather than sacking out he is now feeling me squeeze my butt then through to my thighs, down to my calf and lastly into my spur.

The time it takes to squeeze from my butt down into my spur is only 3 or 4 seconds, it is important that you don't just squeeze the whole lot together. Naturally, he won't know what all of that means, he may even think I am asking him to trot on, some actually do break into the trot. I allow him to speed up, that works in my favour so that

I can teach him to slow down but it all happens in a few seconds. When I say I let him trot off I only allow him a few strides.

So now I am riding him with my full leg and a little spur on him. He hasn't stopped, I leave my legs where they are, I will then reach down with one hand grabbing my reins at the wither (remember, the reins are draped), I lift my hand up fairly high, around about my shoulder height. I don't bring the reins toward my shoulder's, I lift them straight up off his wither.

With my free hand I will close my fist around the reins at or very near the wither, this will give me direct hand to mouth contact with him as it takes up all of the slack.

I leave that same pressure on my legs and spurs, I ask him to back through that pressure in a very positive back up, not a nice, soft couple of steps back, he has to back up very solidly and a fair way back.

Dependant on how this horse backs for me I will gauge how far back he has to back and how strongly he has to back. When I feel he has backed the way I wanted him to, I will simultaneously relax my legs, drop my hands, drape the reins. He has to stop, if he walks forward once I release my hold on him I quickly go through the motions again but this time he gets to back even further. I will sit for about 8 or 10 seconds, let him have a think about what just happened. If he backs quite freely and has no argument about going back, I will stop him after 4 or 5 back strides, I then repeat from the beginning.

I don't turn and go back to the long side of my arena, this will only give him a breather from the exercise and will in turn take longer to teach. If we happen to be in the middle of the arena or nearly at the other side of the arena, that is where I recommence the exercise.

Here are the stages of the exercise:
- Begin with a draped rein, sack out legs for the walk cue

- Work through your squeezing from your butt – thighs – calf – spurs in that order
- Hold the grip in your legs while you pick your draped reins up fairly high with one hand
- With your free hand close your fist around the reins at about the wither
- Take up the slack in the reins and ensure you have direct hand to mouth contact
- Back your horse in a meaningful back, don't dilly-dally here. Keeping the same pressure in your leg/spur squeeze
- Stop your horse, immediately release leg and rein pressure, wait for about 10 seconds and repeat.

Some of the quirky things that your horse may do once he starts to realise your grip in your legs are NOT wanting him to go forward or faster:

- Back in a tight circle
- Try to drift off to the side
- He may stop, bring his head up trying to sort out what this all means, trying to look back at you.

You might think you have broken something

When you get to this stage of the training, you may find that when you try to sack him out with your calves to start off, he won't move. This is totally normal. Don't get angry at him for this…

After all, as the rider, we have created this not wanting to move.

A lot of times, when we are teaching our horse's something, we create a mistake whilst we are trying to fix something totally non-related.

You need to know, this happens and, in my opinion should happen lots of times, it means you are not trying to get your horse to do a hundred things at once and do all those hundred things correctly.

It's quite normal and as long as you are mindful of the mistake you created you can come back and fix it.

To fix it

Keep sacking your horse out with your calves, clucking to him at the same time. Be sure your reins are at a drape. If you are still having trouble getting him to walk forward, don't get tougher with your spurs or heels – bump faster. If he still doesn't compute, lightly steer him in one direction or the other. This will help him move on because he will have to catch himself when you get him off balance.

As soon as your horse moves off stop sacking him out immediately and bring your legs onto him. Starting at the lighter end of the scale, because you want to keep your horse soft and light. If you were to put your legs on from your butt to your heel with full pressure, you will bring him back down to a stop and that is exactly what we teach them to do with this exercise but now, we need to show him how to "ride through the break".

Riding the brake

You will probably find that your horse will be a bit stilted with his movement. He will stop and start, he will hesitate, maybe even lift his head, they tend to lift their head to look back at you for guidance. Don't worry about any of this mess that's going on underneath you, it is definitely fixable.

You've got to be on the ball, really zoned in to his movement. When he hesitates, you have to immediately start sacking him out, use the voice cue "walk on" – at the same time, squeeze your butt cheeks and thighs to hold him from going too fast. This is what I call "riding through the break".

You will have to gauge your leg pressure and use it accordingly. You should find that this will iron out his hesitated, stilted walk/stop/walk movements.

What speed do you walk at?

With any training, I like to over-exaggerate both my cues and my horse's movement. When training at home, your horse will most likely be more laid back than what he would be if he was in a class. We want to train them to walk in a slow, flat footed walk for the class. If you trained that same speed at home you will most likely lose it in the show pen.

The speed you want to train him at home will be extra slow, he will stop and hesitate but this is where you push (it is way better to push your horse than to pull on your horse) on, and then slow him back down again. If, at any time, he pushes through your pressure, you go back to picking up your reins off the wither, squeezing through your legs, backing him up through the squeeze. Repeat everything that you taught him. Once you have got him stopped and you are sitting there relaxed, sack your calves on his sides and squeeze your butt cheeks and thighs, only enough to slow him down, not stop.

As time moves on and with repetition, your horse should lock in with the rhythm of your calves gently sacking him out. Then when you want to stop him, he should stop with a squeeze of your bum cheeks and a little thigh.

Hey Presto! No more spur stopping!...

Only to be used for 'Plan B'.

Cadence at the jog

There's nothing better than riding a Western Pleasure horse that has a cadenced jog. It's just not fun to ride a horse when their too-fast, strung-out jog makes you feel like you have to pull on him all the time. Feeling like you have to be at his face all the time with your reins to slow him down. Pleasure horses are not supposed to be lapping other horses in the pen.

Riders whose horses that are too fast are going to be pulling on the horse's mouth and holding pressure to try and keep them from speeding along. I can see the profile now. The horse has their chin behind the vertical, the reins are super straight from the rider's hands to the horse's mouth, there is no presence in the horse's way of moving underneath, dragging the back end and pulling with the front. What happens when you release those reins and try "show" again? Your horse goes off like a stone out of a sling shot – you pull back, take the movement away – you release your reins and he goes back to his way of going which is too fast because once you turn him loose he falls back onto his shoulders that are going to be dropped which pushes him along in a down-hill fashion.

Getting a winning jog on your horse doesn't come from pulling the reins, slowing your horses jog comes from driving your horse up which creates a deeper stride from behind, this then elevates the shoulders and slows it all down. Doing this creates cadence in your horse.

Jogging your horse, take contact with your horse's mouth by lifting the reins and holding them evenly with both hands. Bumping your legs in a rhythmic fashion, driving him up into the bit. Having contact on the reins and bumping him with your legs is going to get him to lift his belly, come off his shoulders, drive from behind and hold his frame more rounded as opposed to stringing out and dragging his back feet behind him. It will help strengthen his top line which in turn will give him cadence in his jog. As you bump your legs, this action drives his hind end deeper underneath himself.

It may take you a bit of working out how much rein pressure v. leg bumping and squeezing to get it right.

- Too much rein your horse will break down to a walk
- Too much bumping/sacking out will make your horse trot on too fast.

This exercise is more successful if you are repetitious with it. Keep repeating the lift and drive, if he softens, lifts his shoulders and rounds himself up, release the hold, if he speeds up repeat. You need to release now and again to help him gain "natural" cadence.

Your lifting and driving will over time, deepen his stride from behind. It is a great exercise for horses that tend to leave the back legs out behind them when they jog.

In combination, keep contact with his mouth, bump him with your legs and be sure to squeeze a little with your seat and upper legs, *remember, ride the brake,* breaking at the knee so that you can once again sack him out/bump him with your lower legs.

Each time you lift your horse's front end with the reins be sure you are bumping or sacking with your legs in a rhythm with his jog, you never want to hold his face with the reins and ride with no leg, you have got to be using your legs, this is what operates the drive from behind and creates lift, if you didn't use your legs he will simply keep dragging his hind legs lazily along behind him, as soon as you release your hold on his face he will drop his shoulders back down and slop along with no cadence or lift what-so-ever.

Remember, if you release your hold on the reins and he speeds up, repeat the lift, drive up into the bit each time he speeds up. Doing this, you will be able to gradually get him to jog on a draped rein, only using your seat and legs – not your reins.

This is also a strength exercise for your horse. Be patient with him while he strengthens up. He will get stronger at it and will be able to manage to hold his frame and cadence for longer periods of time. Work your horse in both directions, spending more time on his weaker side.

Add this to your tool box

If, by chance, you are still having difficulty slowing your horse down with lifting and driving, you can put him in a fairly decent size circle and when you lift your reins and bump with your legs, shift your inside leg behind the girth and push his hips to the outside of your circle for quite a few strides. (You may have to build up to "quite a few strides"). Not only will you achieve even more deep drive from behind, you will take some of his forward away from him. Any time you push the hips off the track you are tracking on, it takes away some of his speed.

Trail

Pam and SVQ Cashed Up

Training for success in trail starts with taking your time at home, start slow teaching all of the cues you need to manoeuvre through all of the obstacles. Like any other discipline, a trail horse should not be allowed to anticipate and perform the pattern of an obstacle. He should not be allowed to tackle any of the obstacles through habit. When horse's start anticipating an obstacle it becomes a disaster, you will be trying to navigate the obstacle how you see it, your horse will want to tackle it in the way that he has been repetitively trained to perform the obstacle. It will become a hot mess which will cost you the class.

A good trail horse enjoys picking their way through obstacles in the class, they have good expression and body language. They are a real pleasure to ride and really good for the spectators to watch.

Riding a trail pattern will add variety to your horse's life as a show horse especially when you change your trail course at home on a regular basis.

Obstacles are also beneficial for the rider, helping to hone in on your cues. When practicing trail at home, you will discover that you may be pushing too hard with your leg cue when cornering an L shaped back through, sending your horse over the top of the log rather than cornering in between the logs due to too much leg pressure coming from you. You will gain more 'feel' in your cues when you practise with your horse through all of the obstacles.

Having read through this book, outlining the workouts that you will give your horse on a daily basis, both you and your horse will have the ability and the know how to successfully manoeuvre your horse through any of the obstacles.

Poles

Poles can be elevated or on the ground, so It is a good idea to make sure you have some poles elevated at home so that you can work on ensuring your horse will lift his feet when he moves over them. Poles are spaced accordingly for the walk or jog-over, further apart for a lope-over at a show, however, I like to place the poles unevenly at home. This teaches a horse to look for the logs so that he can move over them without standing on top of a log or rolling or clunking them. A horse that stands on, rolls or clunks a pole a few times begins to look for where the poles are placed pretty quickly.

Lightly ticking a pole is usually not counted heavily against a competitor, but knocking a pole over or moving a ground pole is more serious. Walking or jogging the poles with a loose rein, giving the impression of doing it without much guidance makes for a pretty picture. A lope-over, however, calls for more of a collected frame, with light contact. This is where your leg cues to slow and frame up will be very handy to you here. You can put into practice your "riding through the brake" by using your legs and not too much rein.

When training the lope over poles at home, I like to use a large "pin-wheel" or circle of poles and/or a long line of poles set out. I prefer to use both methods together, I will lope the pin-wheel for 5 or 6 revelations then swing over at the lope and lope over the long line of lope poles, loping back into the pin-wheel for a few circles then finish off loping down the line of poles.

You notice I didn't mention stopping between the two obstacles or slow down to a walk or trot. This is important because staying in the lope the whole time will get your horse working and thinking. Your horse needs to start concentrating on his foot fall, when he knows that he won't be stopping so that you can re-set the precise distance of the lope poles and that you will be continuing over them no matter how messy it gets (sometimes it can look like a giant Pick-up-sticks game on the ground), your horse begins to lock in to you, he establishes a rhythm as he continues at the lope. Your horse will try harder if he is kept moving no matter how messy it gets than if you were to stop and re-set the poles every-time he knocks one off line.

When you are ready for practicing the lope poles at the correct show distance, you need be able to accurately judge a horse's length of stride. For poles that are set in a fan shape, a horse with a shorter stride should head for the section where the poles are closer together. Horses with longer strides should perform the obstacle further to the outside of the fan. To successfully negotiate lope-over poles.

Get the approach right and the rest will follow. If you get the approach wrong, the horse will do any of these – drop a stride, take an extra one, switch leads or hit poles.

Gate

I think manoeuvring the gate can be a little "plain Jane" if it is approached, walked through and closed…no big deal, right? If you want to score above everyone else at the gate, put in a bit of showmanship. I mean, rather than just walking up to the gate, walk up *on a loose rein,* this will be dependent on how the gate obstacle has been laid out in the course as to how and where you will end up approaching it, however, if you approach the gate front on, you can stop a couple of strides before you get to the gate to lift the rope, begin to shift your horse into a parallel position a couple of strides off the gate, this way you can show your horse off with a couple of side-pass strides to the latch. Still on a loose rein, use your legs to hold your horse still whilst you unhook the gate.

Now if you have positioned yourself correctly, you should be able to back your horse one stride (with your legs), place your outside leg on and move your horse's shoulder in toward the opening of the gate, walk through heading slightly to the back of the gate just a step so that you know your horses hindquarters will be free from bumping into the gate. Be sure not to go further than a step or two otherwise you will need to back your horse to reach the latch. Getting on the other side of the gate within reach of the latch will have you making less moves than you need to.

Practice moving your horse's hip over a touch just as you are clearing the gate. Doing this will have you close to the gate which will have you looking very professional and your horse polished. It won't be necessary to lean your body as much if at all toward the latch which is part of the reason why your horse will swing his hindquarters away from the gate and make it even harder for you to reach the latch, especially when he thinks the unintentional cue you are giving him with your legs is saying back up.

Be careful to open the gate wider than necessary, this will help you in getting your horse through the gate cleanly. When you have finished the obstacle, side-pass a couple of steps away from the gate to ensure your horse clears the gate.

The above manoeuvres can be dependent on how the gate is to be performed and what else is about the gate, you may have a pole on the other side of the gate for a back through. This will put a damper on your plans of side-passing. But mainly, keep in your mind what sort of horsemanship you can do when manoeuvring the gate obstacle and be sure to practice all of your ideas at home before attempting them at a show.

Bridge

You can practice the bridge a million times at home, with different obstacles around it, different colours and plants, whatever you can think up to "bridge break" your horse.

The old saying...

"if you could have only shown at home you would have won the class".

A good percentage of horses will have some form of curiosity, weariness, suspicion of a bridge at a show. That is why it is imperative that a good trail horse move forward willingly, even if he is feeling a little suspicious. Remember, if your horse takes a step back it is a refusal, so you must have your horse trained to take the bridge with forward motion. I don't mean to rush at the bridge but to have equal foot-fall of a steady, slow, four beat, forward moving walk.

I like a horse that looks at the bridge. I don't want one to go over the bridge like it's not even there, that he is just continuing his walk.

To teach a horse at home to look at the bridge with expression, I will stop my horse and while he is standing still, I will squeeze both of my legs on his sides. At the same time, I have a bit of contact on the reins to encourage him to pull down toward the ground.

Depending on the horse, this may take several attempts to get them to pull down toward the ground, if they show even a slight shift downward I release the hold on the reins and the squeeze in my legs immediately and reward my horse with a pat (small one □). Hopefully, in no time at all, my horse will lower his head and neck with the squeeze of my legs, my reins will be draped.

Now that my horse has this new trick in his tool box, I will then take him to the bridge and stop. (Try not to let your horse stop at the bridge while you are competing, keep walking at the approach). I will have him lower his head then I will walk him over the bridge. I do this three, to four times before I start getting him to lower his head about four strides away from the bridge, this way I can keep him walking, he will lower his head a couple of strides off the bridge and walk over the bridge showing interest in it. I can usually count on greater expression from the horse's when we are approaching the bridge in a class.

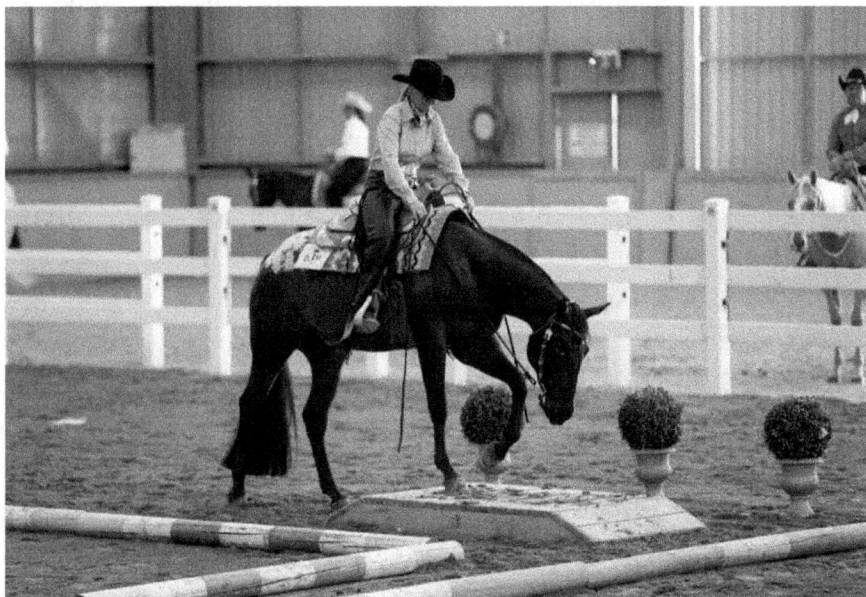

GK Skip On Over, Appaloosa Victorian State Show and Pam Neal

Back-Through

Again, your 'workouts' that you have taught your horse from this book will help you out no end here. Backing your horse through poles is quite basic, it is actually the anxiety and nerves coming from the rider that causes most riders to over cue, going from one spur to the other trying to straighten up – it's happened to us all but when you think about how easy a backup is to manoeuvre, it's got to be the nerves. The horse will pick up on your anxiety and nervousness then you will find yourself in another hot mess.

When training at home I always start with extra-large back throughs, I won't put a horse through the Rule Book size that he will attempt at a show until they have mastered the XL back through at home several times. I feel like this gives them confidence and takes that claustrophobia feel away from them. I still train them as if they are in the show pen so that they are well and truly used to my legs positioning them. It would be of no use if I acted accordingly to the large area, being soft and gentle with my legs and spurs then suddenly I am using my cues in a more demanding, pronounced manner at a show.

You can walk your horse through the back-through a couple of times before you ask them to do the obstacle from the beginning, this will help them get used to being inside the back-through before he has to actually back through it.

Always make sure that you line your horse up straight at the start of the back through. Sit for a couple of seconds to settle. When you begin your back up don't lean forward to look at the poles, wherever you sit your weight your horse has to try and re-balance himself under you, it throws him off balance, he needs to go hunting for you to catch your weight. It's ok to glance down before you begin or stop and glance down then continue on.

Cones

Cones can be another obstacle that can catch a rider out. They are a fairly easy obstacle. As long as you can keep your horse moving fluently at the jog, keeping the same speed and keeping nice, rounded turns. If you try to take the cones in a straighter line or sharper than a smooth, rounded turn you run the risk of your horse getting out of tempo, losing his cadence and breaking gait. A horse that is balanced through many months of 'calisthenic exercises' is much easier to control their speed around the cones than one that is strung out.

Practice jogging your horse slowly through tighter cones at home. While going around the cones, lift and drive your horse through them remembering to keep your turns smooth and rounded. Bump with your legs and drive him into the bit by holding the reins up from his wither with enough contact on his face. This will make it a breeze when you get to the show and the cones are further apart.

Side-pass

The side-pass used to be a burr in my blanket until I read somewhere in an article, that when you are lining up the pole for the side-pass to make sure the pole was aligned behind the rider's heel and ahead of the back cinch, if you ride with a back cinch. Unlike the back-through, it is necessary to look down in the direction of your travels while side passing. Keeping that pole behind your heel will let you know that neither his front or his hindlegs are nearing the pole.

Make your side-pass smooth and flowing, try keeping your horse's body lined up across the poles. You may have to manoeuvre an L shaped side-pass at times so be sure to practice the L shape poles as well.

Hunter in Hand

Hunter in hand is a class geared towards the suitability for Hunter under saddle, creating the perfect venue for many performance-type horse's the chance to be recognized "in hand" for their conformation, and movement.

The horse will approach the judging area (A) and set up for inspection in the "open" position, which means all four legs are visible by the judge when set up for inspection. You will be judged on movement with a maximum score of 70%, 20% conformation and 10% temperament.

Horses' are then asked to first perform a ground covering walk around the smaller triangle A.B.C.A, once complete they swiftly, without hesitation move into an open trot that showcases their movement on the large triangle A.D.E.A. Horses' are expected to move around the triangle with ease, comfort, and a quiet relaxed & natural headset suitable for their body type. At the completion of judging, the handler will lead the horse away from the judging area promptly.

HUNTER IN HAND

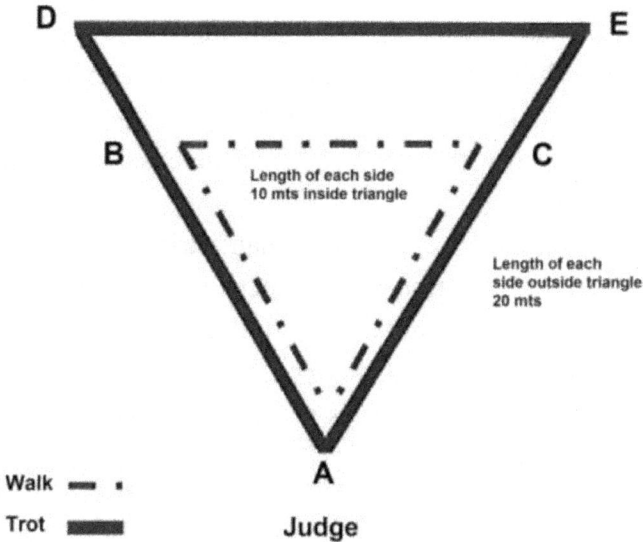

D, E (top corners)
B, C (inside triangle corners)

Length of each side
10 mts inside triangle

Length of each
side outside triangle
20 mts

Walk ━ ▪
Trot ▮▮▮

A

Judge

- An English bridle is mandatory on horses two years old and over after the 1st April. Decorative bridles and halters are prohibited. Bridle must have Egg butt snaffle, D-ring snaffle, O-ring snaffle or full cheek snaffle bit with keepers
- For horses one year old and younger, halters are mandatory. The halter and lead must be of plain leather.

The Handler's attire:

- A collared polo shirt or collared dress shirt, minimum of a short sleeve, must be white or black, no patterns
- Dress pants must be cream, brown, blue or black and be loose enough in which to run. Jodhpurs can be worn; No jeans
- Running shoes must be worn, elastic sided paddock boots or top boots
- Vest and ties (no patterns) gloves and hats are optional.
- If you wear a belt it must be plain.

Many people new to Hunter in hand make the mistake of treating the class as if it is a pattern class similar to showmanship; but this is not the case! The absolute goal is to create the most desirable, fluid and complimenting movement of the horse, and secondly the handler. Learn to match your horse's stride, help them rate their speed with yours, and find the exact speed that your horse looks best at.

Some horses are big, with giant strides meaning their handler has to practically sprint, whilst others might be more ideal at a soft, controlled pace. The horse's headset should be natural and relaxed coming out from the withers. You also want your horses throat latch to be open, and not appear as if the handler is pulling on their horse to slow them down.

Teaching your Hunter Under Saddle horse

When competing in hunter under saddle, you want to get your horse to "stretch" in a hunter frame, they need to learn to go long and low.

I get this elegant look by working my horse at a trot, using both reins, I will slide my hands in the opposite direction to each other starting from just above the horse's wither, ending at a distance of about 12 inches in total, if you had a ruler in your back pocket, you could fit it in between both hands – I'd like to see that!

What I want out of this is to take a hold on my horse's face, making certain that there is no movement at all in my hands. I have definite contact with his mouth at this time, my hands are holding firm and still which takes concentration while the rest of my body is going through the motions of posting to the trot.

As I sink into the saddle which is the downward position of the post, I close my legs and heels on my horse's sides. As I rise to the trot, I relax my legs slightly along with removing my heels, however, I will not change the pressure on my "wide" position of my hands, or the hold on my horse's face until I feel a downward pull in my reins. As soon as I feel this downward pull, be it ever so slightly, I will release my hold and resume my correct position with my hands on the reins back at the wither with light hand to mouth contact. I will repeat this hand and leg action which encourages the horse to come off my hand contact and stretch his head and neck down (not in) while continuing to have good engagement behind. I think too much attention is put on a horse's under carriage, which don't get me wrong is very important but rider's also need to think about where they are placing their horse's head and neck position. I do not want to bring a horse's head and neck toward my hands, I don't want to see an arch in his neck or the nose being behind the vertical.

Figure 1. *English Rubber Snaffle*

A hunter should go in a longer, lower frame with light contact (not loose contact) at all the gaits. Once they learn to stretch down at the trot, they will also understand the concept at the walk and canter as well. The picture above shows my most favourite bit (in English). It is a Rubber D ring snaffle and it is the bee's knees, it fixes a myriad of problems and is kind at the same time. It is a Lorina Rubber Snaffle and is the best by far for getting your hunter horse long and low.

The picture below is of myself and SVQ Cashed Up. We are warming up for a class at the National Pleasure Horse Association show, N.S.W., I think around 2010 but don't hold me to it. Anyway, the picture is a good example, you will see my hands are opening up away from each other, I am in the process of getting Hooch to reach down with his head and neck, I like how he is also opening up in the area of his throat latch and he is in no way behind the vertical.

SVQ Cashed Up and Pam Neal

The Ranch Horse

The purpose of the ranch pleasure class is to measure the ability of the horse to be a pleasure to ride while being used as a means of conveyance from performing one property horse task to another. The horse should reflect the versatility, attitude and movement of a working horse riding outside the confines of an arena. The horse should be well trained, relaxed, quiet, soft and cadenced at all gaits. The ideal ranch horse will travel with forward movement and demonstrate an obvious lengthening of stride at extended gaits. The horse can be ridden with light contact or on a relatively loose rein without requiring undue restraint, but not shown on a full drape of reins. The overall manners and responsiveness of the ranch pleasure horse to make timely transitions in a smooth and correct manner, as well as the quality of the movement are of primary considerations. The ideal ranch pleasure horse should have a natural head carriage at each gait. Horses shall be shown individually and the class may be conducted inside or outside of an arena. (AQHA 2018).

Professor Sumner Miller & Trace Paterson

I am a self-confessed poser, so when ranch riding became a thing in competition, I was not drawn to it at first because you can't "bling up" your horse by banding manes, clipping ears and adding in a false tail. Silver accessories on saddles and bridles is discouraged and that's before I get to blinging up myself! I believe the bling is the reason why I fell in love with western pleasure in the first place. It's just my jam I suppose and everyone is different...I love the bling, the slow, cadenced lope, the sparkling like a disco ball as the pleasure horse moves down the rail on a draped rein.

Ranch riding has become increasingly popular, drawing huge numbers of keen riders to its classes. I guess you can still put on a pose in ranch riding classes. ☐ There's a multitude of reasons why Ranch Riding is one of the fastest-growing classes at the shows. This class isn't about bling or pizzazz. Instead, it rewards a solid, well-broke horse that shows most suitable for getting the job done on a working ranch, a horse that rides and works with purpose.

The first thing you need to know about ranch pleasure, it is not western pleasure. A western pleasure horse is rewarded for calm, collected gaits performed on a loose rein, whereas a ranch pleasure horse has a forward-moving style that looks as if he has somewhere to go. The ranch horse needs to look like he needs to get somewhere and cover a lot of ground, he is after all working on a ranch and needs to get his job done that includes being able to navigate the land safely.

When showing your horse in ranch pleasure, your reins should have a little slack in them but not a drape like in western pleasure, they can have a small drape, however, should be short enough for you to have ready contact when you need it. A ranch pleasure horse should go with his nose slightly out and his neck elevated a little, you still want him relatively flat and level in his neck, but also looking where he's going. Control is crucial because of all the transitions in Ranch Riding, you should have good control of the walk, trot and lope, and also be able to show off some speed variations, such as extension at these three gaits.

Ease up on your hands

Your seat is the closest form of communication you can have with your horse. You want to control your horse's body so learn to control it through your seat and legs, not all from your hand.

Don't mistake extension for going fast

Extending a gait doesn't mean "go fast." It means the horse should extend the reach of his legs to cover more ground.

Back to Calisthenic Exercises

The workout exercises that you will have read in *"Your daily workout routine"* are designed to develop body control and strength in any discipline and on any horse, you choose to ride so don't leave them out for the ranch horse. These exercises will soften your horse for you:

- counter arc/bend;

- side-passing;

- two tracking;

- move the shoulders;

- move the hips;

- walk, jog and lope in serpentines;

- walk, jog and lope over some poles;

Note: When moving the hip, keep both his face and hip to the same side (that will be the outside). Pushing the hip the same direction as the face will help keep your horse from dropping in the shoulders.

Just about any horse and rider can compete in ranch pleasure as long as they have these basics already in place:

- The ability to move off the rider's leg and rein;

- The ability to lope off in the correct lead.

Glossary

Long Two -Year- Old: A two-year-old that is nearing the end of his two-year-old year. Yearlings nearing the end of their yearling year are also referred to as Long Yearlings.

Draped Rein: When you have very light hand to mouth contact, you're riding with a loose rein, the reins are in a 'U' shaped drape.

Sacking out with your legs: Like bumping with your legs. You may be holding with your seat and thighs but from your knee down, your lower leg is ever so slightly swinging away and back onto your horse's side. Sacking out with your lower legs aids in relaxing a young green broke horse, it helps them follow the rhythm and also lets them know you are still there and all is well. If you leave your legs still on a green horse, they are more inclined to spook when you do eventually move your leg to cue them in any way.

Climber: A climber is a horse that is restricted from moving forward freely. The rider holds the horse back with their legs and spurs holding onto the horse's sides and asking the horse to "ride through the brake" whilst loping. The horse is artificially held back and finds itself with nowhere else to go but climb with its front end. He develops an over-exaggerated bend in his knee, giving the impression that he is climbing a hill.

Ground time/Air time: The amount of time a horse will hold the ground for before they leave it is ground time and the amount of time a horse's leg/legs are in the air before touching the ground is air time.

Ride through the brake: This term is when you have a degree of hold on your horse with your legs however, you are pushing him through the hold with your lower leg or heel/spur. You can be using both of these actions at the same time or flow from one to the other instantaneously when you feel your horse speeding up you can add a bit of thigh to slow them down but at the same time be gently pushing him on with a bump, bump action in your lower leg to ensure the horse holds his tempo. *Similar to the term Drive into the bit which you can read next...*

Drive into the bit: This is similar to Riding Through the Brake. To drive your horse into the bit means that you will have direct contact from your hands to your horse's mouth, holding the reins up from his wither not down and back toward your belly while at the same time you bump with your legs to push him up. The horse has nowhere to go but concertina himself toward the bit. When this happens, it encourages him to lift his shoulders and drive his back legs underneath himself.

Hiding behind the bit: The horse will appear intimidated by the riders' hands, he will travel with his neck arched and with a stiff appearance, his chin will be behind the vertical. This not only shows up with hand to mouth contact, it can also be displayed when on a loose rein. As mentioned in the above sentence, it is also known as being behind the vertical because the horse's chin is closer to its chest rather than being level or slightly in front of the vertical.

Look through the bridle: When a horse is travelling on a loose rein in a relaxed but alert manner and is enjoying the job at hand, he will be more inclined to prick his ears forward and show lots of nice expression and interest. He looks as if he is "looking" at something in the distance. Saying "through the bridle" mean's he is not turning his head this way and that, looking all around him, he is simply looking forward – through the bridle.

Cadence: The marked accentuation of the rhythm and (musical) beat that is a result of a steady and suitable tempo harmonizing with a springy impulsion.

For cadence, if you look up the actual definition of the word, especially those relating to music, it does make sense in a riding usage. It is rhythm but it's also the "phrasing", the emphasis, if you like. So, the footfalls are in the same timing but also in the same strength.

Downhill: Most horses tend to want to carry their weight on the front end. When you study a horse that carries most of his weight up front, you will want to say that he looks like he is travelling "downhill" that is because the horse is "leaning" forward. A horse should be continually trained to get their weight off their front end. Once this is accomplished, the horse lifts from the shoulder and appears to be "upright", when upright he is more "cadenced".

Trope: A horse that tropes is jogging on his hindquarters and loping on his forehand. They tend to also have a rocking motion in their hips rocking from left to right. You can pick this by standing behind the horse and watching him *"lope/trope"* away from you – it shows up in their tails moving from one side to the other, a bit like wiggling their tails.

A trope usually comes from the rider not correcting their horse's way of going once the horse has locked in to the trope, it is easier for them to travel this way by trotting from behind and pulling their back end along with the forelegs along with their backs not being rounded. To the rider that allows this to happen, its slow up there on the horse's back so that must mean there's nothing to fix, they're going slow, just sit there and show!

Over-Canting: When the horse's outside hind is beyond the inside front lead leg. Over-canting gives the impression that the horse is "Crabbing" down the rail. His head and neck will be facing the rail, his shoulders are not travelling square down the rail. Some rider's like to over-cant because it slows the horse's forward movement down.

Self-carriage: A horse's ability to properly carry himself, similar to good posture in people. He's responsible for his own carriage and doesn't rely on his rider to hold him in the proper position. He should be holding his shoulders up while keeping his back rounded, and he's maintaining collection.

Counter-arc: A counter-arc which is also known as a counter bend is when your horse is travelling in one direction, however, his head and neck will be positioned in the opposite direction. The reason you want to do this in your daily workouts is to work on lifting their shoulder's. Horse's tend to want to carry most of their weight on the forehand so we need to continually correct this and be persistent at it. If we only get their shoulder's up now and again, they won't learn "Self-Carriage" (*see above "self-carriage"*).

Bibliography

AQHA. 2018. "Rule Book."

Foster, A. n.d. *Products.* Antoinette Foster. Accessed March 12, 2019. www.hiform.com.au.

Oregon, Uni. n.d. *ir.library.oregonstate.edu.* Accessed 3 12, 2019. ir.library.oregonstate.edu.

Wells, C. 2009/10 "Clinic".

Ourimbah Vet website – www.ourimbahvet.com.au. Vaccines

Valley Equine website – www.valleyequine.com.au. Vaccines

PubMed – ncbi.nlm.nih.gov. Potential role of maternal lineage in the thoroughbred breeding strategy.

About the Author

Born in Ireland and immigrating to Australia when she was two with her mum, dad, two sisters and three brothers. Arriving by ship and berthing in Perth, Western Australia. From Perth Pam and her family took the long trek East by train. Eventually, the family settled in Altona in Victoria. And so, began Pam's life as a little Aussie girl.

The family rented for a while until they were able to move in to a brand new three bed-room brick home right next to Altona Golf Course and only minutes from the beach.

The area where they settled was known as "The Bird Cage" because the streets were named after birds. It was a family friendly area, the streets were all gravel back then, all the kids in the street would play together until they were rounded up for tea. There was an army of them!

Being a relatively new area, there were lots of vacant blocks, the kids that owned horses had their dads put up fences on all of these vacant blocks and that was where they kept their ponies and the kids that missed out simply tethered them on the big median strip that went from the shops all the way down to the edge of the golf course, it was probably only a half a mile in length but when you are a little kid, that's pretty big

Pam realised her love for horses when she was 5. She claims to remember the time as she had only just started school.

There were horses living in vacant blocks and tethered all over the place in town. None of the kids could afford acreage back then. The kids that had horses would ride them to school, tether them for the day while they were in school, they would sling a plastic bucket over their arm to bring for their water.

Every available chance Pam could get she would sneak out and hop on one of the horses, even if they were lying down, she would get on them and cuddle them. Of a night she would sneak out and harass these poor ponies that just wanted to sleep or eat. Pam wanted to ride high in the saddle and fight some Indians!

Pam had met her Soul Mate George who was walking down the middle of the road to take her horse from her, he had bought the pony from Pam's mum that day and was now coming to claim it. At the time neither Pam nor George even dreamt they would be a couple, after all, Pam was only 9 at the time. Jumping a few years on from there after They got married and moved out into their own home. Pam had bought her first show horse while they were living in Werribee South. He was a very eye-catching Liver Chestnut colt. Her first halter class with him was at a small western show in the town of Lara in Victoria. They won the yearling halter that day and went Grand Champion. From there it just got better.

Pam began playing around with showing Quarter Horse's, Appaloosa's and Paints for many years. It wasn't until she and her husband moved to a little country town on the West side of Ballarat called Snake Valley that she became a Professional Trainer and Rider Coach she began operating her breeding and training facility, Snake Valley Quarter Horses.

Pam laughed as she explained how her and George ended up in Snake Valley, George had fallen off his camel Kaboobi, he broke his leg in two places and the only doctor about that day was a Gynaecologist! Needless to say, he had to have his leg re-broken down the track and have it properly re-set because it just wouldn't heal. So, what do you do with a guy that is lying around in bed with his broken leg looking out of the window at Kaboobi in the front paddock? You go for lots of road trips.

Somehow, they ended up in Snake Valley, where they fell in love with the place, bought some land and went about building their beautiful Bluestone home and their lives. Not only were they breeding horses, they also farmed Fallow deer for many years.

Before Pam became a trainer, she used a couple of trainers, "Trainers are trainers, right?", she said "I wasn't a trainer and the old saying - One man, one job".

Things didn't go to plan". Pam says she knows what it's like for amateur's, she used to be one and uses that insight when she is giving lessons or clinics.

Pam thanks those trainers because if it wasn't for them, she wouldn't have become a trainer herself. She decided to take a-hold of the reins (pun intended) and get the job done the way she wanted it done. From there on Pam says she never looked back.

Alongside breeding, training and campaigning her stud's progeny, (Chicks Impressive Charm, Assets N Cash), she also trained for the public. They say "*You're only as good as the horse underneath you*", Pam can certainly say she had some 'pearler' horses under her.

Her showing career was a very successful one for both herself and for her client's. She said, "*The* best moments were definitely watching my clients along with my husband George win and place high in their events. Whether it was a local "A" show or a major show throughout Australia and New Zealand. To see the excitement and elation on their faces was worth every minute of my 32-year training career".

Pam, George and Kiwi. George's turn at having a strapper.

Easter 2016 was Pam's forced retirement.

"I had a new batch of young two-year old's in work, I was training them up for that year's show season.

One particular filly that had a bit of spook in her had already bucked me off once then went about jumping all over my left leg. She had got a bit excited about some horses galloping up to and past the arena, I guess she thought it looked alright and maybe she could join in. In the meantime, while she was watching intently at this mixture of horses coming full gallop toward us, other riders' that were there were placing logs on the ground ready for some lessons over the logs, she obviously was oblivious to this going on in the background. I turned her around away from the galloping horses and walked off to start working her, she saw the logs that weren't there a moment ago, stepped awkwardly on one of them and let loose.

I nearly had her, she came to her senses for a short moment but decided she wasn't finished bucking, she got me off then stomped all over me. I can still see the hoof marks on my leg. I healed up really well from that but not so good the next fright she got.

I was finishing up on her, riding along the rail letting my foot tap on the rail. Occasionally tapping the rail with my rein. Nothing that I haven't done before on her or any other horse. This time my boot got stuck behind the post which turned my toe out as I passed by. My spur stuck in her side which she didn't flinch at, she actually did what she thought was what I was asking her to do, she moved her hip toward the centre of the arena, somehow her front-end leant really hard on the railings of the arena, they made this almighty crack! She was fine with that until the colt I had tied up 15 feet away under a tree went crazy, he had been asleep and had been rudely awakened by the almighty crunch. He just about climbed the tree he was tied to. That was enough for my filly I was riding, she backed up out of the broken mess straight into the railing on the other side of the corner we were in smashing them she lunged forward and sideways, propped, then took off in another direction then back again.

Next thing I knew I was lying on the ground not being able to get my breath with an excruciating pain in my upper back.

I had my phone on the ground behind one of the posts to keep it out of the sun. If I had of chosen to put my phone on top of the post, I would probably have snuffed it. I dragged myself over to my phone, rang my husband who told me off for not ringing an ambulance! When one of the two ambulances arrived (I suddenly felt important – who gets two ambo's!) they finally got me in the back of one of the ambulance's, they told me I had a collapsed lung and a broken rib or two. Once I was X-rayed, I had 8 broken ribs and a fractured vertebra along with the collapsed lung.

Three weeks prior, my husband had a heart attack which was brought on by a mould particle out of some old hay. His condition was known as 'Farmers Lung'. George looked at me in the ambulance, I looked back at him and in unison we both said "never again".

That day brought on early retirement for both of us, we were talking about travelling Australia one day after retirement anyway, it just brought the travel date closer."

So now, Pam and George have traded saddles and bridles for fishing rods and Harley's and are travelling Australia, living in a motor home full time, booking clinics and lessons along the way and totally loving their lives, meeting all the riders and their horse's out there in the wild blue yonder.

Thank you!

Thank you for reading my book. I thoroughly enjoyed writing it. Writing this book has brought back many great memories and some not-so-great!

I hope that by reading "From Go To Whoa" that it will help you in your goals of training your own horse. I always say – "Even if you only get one good thing out of your lesson or clinic, it is worth every cent you have paid". I hope the same rings true for this book.

Thank you to all of my clients over the years for choosing me to train and coach your horses and yourselves, I truly appreciate you all.

To a very special lady Antoinette Foster the founder of HiForm Australia, thank you for believing in me, taking me on with sponsorship for many years, your supplements were a cornerstone in the health of not only my horses but my client's horses also. Thank you from the bottom of my heart to you and your team.

My brilliant farriers Bruce O'Dell and Brendan Meagher, definitely two of the best farriers out there.

My equine dentist Darren Lynch, for without you Darren I would have had more trouble than you could ever poke a stick at, you are a magician!

Cliff Marisma my breaker for making sure every horse he had broken-in was as safe as houses before handing them back to me for training – a gutsy, fearless "Crash Test Cowboy"! Thank you so much Cliff.

To my best friend, confidante, number 1 strapper, chef and husband George, I wouldn't have done it without you, 100% sure of that! I love you heaps!

My daughter Sarah for coping with late night dinners and spending every Easter of her childhood and teenage years at Werribee Park Equestrian Centre, hunting eggs in the stables and arena! I love you.

My dear friend and catch rider David Pearce, love you buddy.

All the young girls that have come to work for me over the years helping me with the running of Snake Valley Quarter Horses.

Last but in no way least my best ever house, horse and the rest of the menagerie sitters Sonia Missen and Vicki Bull, you girls were absolutely a God send, I think I can truly say, "I couldn't have done it without you", you're the best.

THE END!

www.ingramcontent.com/pod-product-compliance
Lightning Source LLC
Chambersburg PA
CBHW051821090426
42736CB00011B/1586